FAIRFIELD PORTER
An American Painter

FAIRFIELD

Fairfield Porter in his Southampton Studio. Mid 1960s.
The Fairfield Porter Archives, The Parrish Art Museum

PORTER

AN AMERICAN PAINTER

William C. Agee

with

Malama Maron-Bersin,

Michele White, and Peter Blank

The Parrish Art Museum

Southampton, New York

Fairfield Porter: An American Painter

has been made possible with the generous support of:

Mrs. Jack C. Massey

Mr. Charles Simon

The National Endowment for the Arts,
  Washington, D.C., A Federal Agency

Del Laboratories, Inc.

The Cowles Charitable Trust

Robert Lehman Foundation, Inc.

L & L Foundation

Betty Parsons Foundation

Suffolk County Office of Cultural Affairs

SCHEDULE OF THE EXHIBITION

The Parrish Art Museum
Southampton, New York
June 27 – September 12, 1993

Mead Art. Museum
Amherst College
Amherst, Massachusetts
October 29 – December 24, 1993

The Snite Museum of Art
University of Notre Dame
Notre Dame, Indiana
January 20 – March 20, 1994

Albright-Knox Art Gallery
Buffalo, New York
May 14 – July 3, 1994

Colby College Museum of Art
Waterville, Maine
July 20 – September 21, 1994

Cover: *Painting Materials*, c. 1949
Back cover: *Anne in a Striped Dress*, 1967

CONTENTS

LENDERS TO THE EXHIBITION

Mead Art Museum, Amherst College, Amherst, Massachusetts
The Cleveland Museum of Art, Ohio
Dayton Art Institute, Ohio
Wadsworth Atheneum, Hartford, Connecticut
The Heckscher Museum, Huntington, New York
The Nelson-Atkins Museum of Art, Kansas City, Missouri
Sheldon Memorial Art Gallery, University of Nebraska–Lincoln
The Metropolitan Museum of Art, New York
Whitney Museum of American Art, New York
Pennsylvania Academy of the Fine Arts, Philadelphia
Memorial Art Gallery of the University of Rochester, New York
William A. Farnsworth Library and Art Museum, Rockland, Maine
The Saint Louis Art Museum, Missouri
Santa Barbara Art Museum, California
Rose Art Museum, Brandeis University, Waltham, Massachusetts
Hirshhorn Museum and Sculpture Garden, Smithsonian Institution, Washington, D.C.
The Phillips Collection, Washington, D.C.

Stephen S. Alpert, Boston, Massachusetts
Dr. Marianne de Nagy Buchenhorner, Courtesy Tibor de Nagy Gallery, New York
Arthur M. Bullowa, New York
Constance Jewett Ellis, New York
The Equitable Life Assurance Society of the U.S., New York
Douglas and Beverly Feurring, Boca Raton, Florida
Katherine Koch, Brooklyn, New York
Arlie James Lambert, Bristol, Tennessee
Andre Nasser, New York
Mr. and Mrs. Donald Newhouse, New York
Jane P. Norman, New York
Katharine M. Porter, Atlanta, Georgia
Jane L. Richards, New York
Three Private Collections

Private Collection, Courtesy Alpha Gallery, Boston
Mickelson Gallery, Washington, D.C.

PREFACE

FAIRFIELD PORTER was an artist of an unusual nature. His sensibility was broadly based, and his position was secured through resolve and genuineness. His art was profound enough to enable him to convey complex matters with simplicity. Porter is at once both unpretentious and assertive, conservative and natural, understated and straightforward. Given such attributes, it is not surprising that he has never been fashionable. As William C. Agee has observed, the more we study Porter, the more insistent and the more complex the work becomes.

We are privileged as a museum to have received in 1980 the Fairfield Porter bequest of 237 works of art, and now to have the art historian William C. Agee provide the kind of insight required of Porter's accomplishments and his importance for twentieth-century American painting.

It is interesting to note that Porter shared certain affinities with William Merritt Chase, whose works are also central to our collection. Porter's artistic attitude was influenced by the practices of French Impressionism, as was Chase's, and as mature painters both are distinctly American. In their respective pursuits of representation, we see how light is a determining factor. And as Chase did, Porter played a central role in our community; our holdings are enhanced by these artists whose achievements were grounded in so large a part by their sense of place.

Among the many individuals whom I wish to thank, the distinguished historian William C. Agee must be the first. He has helped us understand Porter anew, and he has guided students and staff alike with a spirit of erudition and inquiry. His presence here is due in large part to Anina Porter Fuller's initial overture, to Anne Porter's wholehearted support, and to the full cooperation of Hunter College, and the Chair of its Department of Art, Sanford Wurmfeld.

Others have been both generous and essential to this effort: Joan Ludman's research for a catalogue raisonné; Hunter College graduate students Malama Maron-Bersin, Michele White, Sara Rosenfeld, and Peter Blank; Alicia Longwell, Registrar; Robert Schumann, Assistant to the Robert Lehman Curator; Anke Jackson, Deputy Director; Kent dur Russell, Curator of Education; Gwen Gaines, Secretary to the Director; Donna De Salvo, Robert Lehman Curator; Martha Stotzky, Education Coordinator; Pat Pickett, Building Manager/Preparator; all of The Parrish Art Museum; Lane Talbot and Betty Cunningham of Hirschl & Adler Galleries, Inc.; Sara Blackburn for her editorial expertise; and Tish O'Connor and Dana Levy of Perpetua Press.

The current exhibition is largely drawn from the Parrish's holdings and enriched by important loans that were secured from private collectors and museums. Many have parted with cherished works, and we are immensely grateful for their good will.

I want to thank our colleagues who will share this presentation with us and whose support was critical to this effort. Our partners are: the Mead Art Museum, Amherst College, Amherst; The Snite Museum of Art, University of Notre Dame, Notre Dame; the Albright-Knox Art Gallery, Buffalo; the Colby College Museum of Art, Waterville, Maine; and the Museum of Art, Fort Lauderdale.

Importantly, our donors made this enterprise possible, and we are especially grateful to the National Endowment for the Arts, Washington, D.C., A Federal Agency; Del Laboratories, Inc.; The Cowles Charitable Trust; Mrs. Jack C. Massey; Mr. Charles Simon; the Betty Parsons Foundation, Inc.; the L & L Foundation; the Robert Lehman Foundation, Inc.; and the Suffolk County Office of Cultural Affairs.

Finally, the Trustees of The Parrish Art Museum have provided the institutional sustenance that has enriched the Parrish's mission and given life to this particular endeavor.

TRUDY C. KRAMER
Director

FOREWORD AND ACKNOWLEDGMENTS

THIS EXHIBITION is the second devoted to Fairfield Porter (1907-1975) which I have organized with the graduate students I teach at Hunter College. Each has taken as its point of departure the collection of 237 works by Fairfield Porter in The Parrish Art Museum in Southampton, New York. The first, a smaller exhibition, was entitled *Porter Pairings*, and was held at the Leubsdorf Art Gallery of Hunter College in the spring of 1992. It consisted of twenty-three paintings by Porter drawn soley from the Museum's collection and was accompanied by a modest catalogue, with an essay and a selection of writings by and about Fairfield Porter. In that show we explored some of the themes and motifs as well as the dualities in Porter's life and art. Its success led us to expand the project into the current exhibition and catalogue, which are considerably larger and more ambitious. Now, twenty-six works from the Parrish collection have been supplemented by thirty-nine loans of paintings dating from 1938 to Porter's death in 1975. Building on the conclusions drawn from the first exhibition, our goal now is to illuminate the nature and extent of Porter's achievement as well as to explore more fully the Porter collection at The Parrish Art Museum by seeing it in the context of the loans secured for this exhibition.

Our in-depth study of the Porter collection at the Parrish—the first such study to have been undertaken—has been a surprisingly rewarding one. It has shown that the collection is far deeper in good and even outstanding paintings than we first realized. We now know that this has to do with the nature of Porter's work, as well as with our perception of it, for Porter's art belies first impressions. What looks easy and casual is in fact difficult and slow to reveal itself. This exhibition contains several paintings which we initially overlooked, thinking them unfinished or irretrievably awkward, even in some cases, crude. It should also be made clear that still more paintings of real merit and interest could not be included in this exhibition because of space limitations. By the same token, the decision not to include watercolors or prints had to be made, but as strong as many of these are, it is Porter's oil paintings which are his most valuable contribution. In the future no doubt other Porter works will continue to reveal themselves in ways not presently apparent to us. Therein lies the first of many lessons found in this collection: Porter can

be as complex, as difficult, and as problematic as any other artist. The vitality of his art—the quality he most respected in any art—ensures that the collection will demand continued study.

A word is in order about how this collection and thus this exhibition came to the Parrish. Fairfield Porter was an important American painter from 1949 until his death in 1975. Not coincidentally, those were the years when he lived in Southampton, New York, the home of the Parrish. The Porters had moved there in 1949 to give their large and growing family ample room, and a place where they could swim in the ocean. In 1949, the Hamptons were only sparsely settled, and afforded a tranquil setting in which Porter could pursue his art. Southampton provided the perfect complement to the long summers the family spent on Great Spruce Head Island in Penobscot Bay, Maine. Porter and his family became deeply attached to the village, and his wife, Anne Channing Porter, a distinguished American poet, still lives there today, a stone's throw from the Museum.

Among the pleasures of Southampton is The Parrish Art Museum, a lively and important institution that has contributed significantly to our understanding of American art since the time of Thomas Moran (1847–1926) and William Merritt Chase (1849–1916), artists who early on had also captured the particular beauty of the eastern Long Island landscape. The Parrish has had a long and deep commitment to living American art and it has always understood the special place held by Fairfield Porter in our art.

In 1980, the estate of Fairfield Porter recognized the bond between the artist, the village, and the Museum by donating 237 of his works in all media to the Museum. In turn, this collection has been subsequently enhanced by other gifts of Porter works. I came to know it on a visit to the Museum several years ago. The Porter collection immediately struck me as a rare resource ideally suited for concentrated research by the Hunter graduate students. Its proximity to such resources is a real strength of the Hunter Art Department, and it has always supported direct student involvement in research projects that have produced exhibitions and catalogues. Porter was not an artist the students in the department or the large college community were likely to know, and just as clearly, he was an artist they should know.

I proposed the idea to Trudy C. Kramer, Director of the Museum, and to Sanford Wurmfeld, Chairperson of the Hunter Art Department and Director of the Hunter Art Gallery. Each enthusiastically supported the project from the beginning. They have lent their full assistance at every turn. Trudy Kramer and her staff have been a delight to work with, and I want to extend my warmest gratitude to all of them. In particular, Alicia Longwell, Registrar, and Pat Pickett, Building Manager/Preparator, have done unstinting and yeoman work with every phase of the exhibition, including moving paintings to and from storage for study; Alicia Longwell also oversaw loans and all details of the exhibition and catalogue. Anke Jackson, Deputy Director, has kept the enterprise on course with her supervision of the project. Kent dur Russell, Curator of Education, and Martha Stotzky, Education Coordinator, have pulled together and overseen all the educational materials and programs with skill and patience. Donna De Salvo, the Museum's Robert Lehman Curator, has offered valuable insights into Porter and the exhibition, and has been unfailing with her support and encouragement. Robert Schumann, Assistant to the Robert Lehman Curator, and Gwen Gaines, Secretary to the Director, have handled innumerable details.

We owe a special debt of gratitude to Joan Ludman, whose inventory of the collection has been indispensable, for her willing assistance and guidance.

We also wish to thank Julie Melby, Librarian of the Whitney Museum of American Art and herself an exceptional student at Hunter, as well as Nancy Malloy and the staffs of the Archives of American Art and The Museum of Modern Art for their invaluable help with our research.

Peter Blank, Malama Maron-Bersin, Michele White, as well as Sara Rosenfeld in the first stage of the project, are the graduate students I enlisted to work with me. They have worked diligently and effectively, and their contributions run throughout the exhibition and catalogue. Peter Blank has prepared the Bibliography and List of Exhibitions; Malama Maron-Bersin has edited the writings by and about Porter; and Michele White has done the Chronology. Together we studied collections and prepared the list of works which have now been brought together. It has been a pleasure to work with them, and we owe them our respect and gratitude. I also want to thank Pam Johnstone, who was a student at Hunter, for her help.

We owe an enormous debt of gratitude to the friends and family of Fairfield Porter for sharing their knowledge and love of him as artist, writer, and as a man. Foremost has been Anne Channing Porter, who was Porter's

wife for more than forty years, and shared her insight and understanding with us with unfailing patience and good humor. It has been a rare and literally unforgetable experience to work with her, and we are very grateful. Porter's niece, Anina Porter Fuller, herself a painter of merit, gave her time and help generously, contributing the insight of another painter. Ted Leigh, a former student of Porter, has generously shared the Porter letters he has lovingly gathered, which offer unique insights. Rackstraw Downes, a fine painter and editor of the indispensible collection of Porter's writings, *Art in Its Own Terms,* which now has been reprinted, has been central to the greatly increased knowledge and understanding we presently have of Porter. His long and deep commitment to Porter and his art has been an inspiration to us, and we hope this catalogue and exhibition will help to further the task he has begun.

Finally, we must express a long and loud voice of thanks to all the collectors and institutions who have been willing to lend their paintings. We have asked a lot of them, and they have responded with great understanding and generosity. We are all grateful to each and every one.

WILLIAM C. AGEE
Professor of Art, Hunter College

9

FAIRFIELD PORTER

AN AMERICAN PAINTER "DENSE WITH EXPERIENCE"

William C. Agee

NOTHING IS AS IT SEEMS on first appearance in either the work or the life of Fairfield Porter (1907-1975). His landscapes, interiors, and portraits are often beautiful and seem genial, but perhaps too polite and certainly not difficult or demanding. Because he was Harvard-educated and independently wealthy, Porter the person may strike us at first in the same way: as an artist who had a life of ease. There are, to be sure, elements of truth in this. Yet the life and art of Fairfield Porter are rich with dualities, apparent contradictions, and even paradoxes. Porter and his art are far more complex than we might first suppose.

Porter is, for example, often called a realist painter.[1] The description is inaccurate, however, for it does not express the true concerns of his work. His paintings convey a strong sense of place and presence, but for him the literal transcription of what he saw before him was "beside the point."[2] The actual subject was of little concern; rather it was in the paint itself that he found the life, the vitality, and the wholeness of the painting. He understood that the difference between realism and abstraction is not as simple as it seems. For Porter, the physical qualities of the medium come first, and it is the tension between realism and abstraction that reveals the essential character of his art. What seems easy and casual in his work in fact often turns out to be complicated, difficult, and even arbitrary. As evidence, we need only to look at *Penobscot Bay with Peak Island* (fig. 34) of 1966. Here Porter rendered a patch of dense Maine fog as a physical, palpable area of paint, more solid than the adjoining land mass, which in turn was cut off sharply and abruptly at the left. Air and space became weighty, the better to serve the needs of the painting as a tangible, concrete fact. Rather than literally describing, Porter determined the relations and connections between things, and for him it was these relations that were the vital elements in a painting.

In his approach and method, Porter sought an unforced natural-ness.[3] The idea was to render the canvas fluently and of a piece, by means of an abstract, interlocking surface; in this way it was the sum of his painterly decisions that determined the composition. Here was how Porter discovered the life and vitality inherent in what he saw, capturing his essential experience of the world around him. To confuse this naturalness with a bland, unthinking art, as we may be likely to do, is a mistake. The "natural" does not just happen. It is a conscious, hard-won position that Porter achieved only over a lifetime. He spent more than twenty years at his craft before he could consistently realize paintings of a high order that could stand with the best art of his time.

His search for a fluent, natural style of painting led Porter to develop a directness that often appears at first, not as easy, but as blunt and even awkward. Thus we can understand why Larry Rivers referred to him as a "flat-footed" painter,[4] and why certain elements are often "off" or seem "wrong" in many of his paintings, even to the extent that we may pass them over the first time around. Such was the case in our study with *Lunch under the Elm Tree* (fig. 10) of 1954. Other paintings, such as *Lizzie, Guitar and Christmas Tree, No. 1* (fig. 58) and *No. 2* of 1973, can be so prickly that they may set the teeth on edge. This is because Porter put down what he needed for a painting, focusing on what occupied him at the moment, and then he would summarily cut it off. He refused to make any concessions to either sentiment or to traditional canons of finish or painterly agility. But our perceptions can change with time, and by being with his pictures. This is another paradox in Porter's art: what seems casual demands long and hard concentration. Porter understood this. He believed that a painting exists in time and changes in time, and like Ingres, he left it to time to finish his paintings. For Porter, things that looked "awkward and out of place you find out are not so awkward. They have their place, and it is an integral and not a scattered thing."[5]

Porter was a reserved man, but he was neither remote nor aloof from the world around him. He had strong political, social, and aesthetic views. He was, for example, a staunch environmentalist at an early date, when this consciousness was far from widespread. The intensity of his commitment to the environmental cause comes through in his love of the land so clearly evident in his work. He was also deeply committed to nuclear disarmament. Early on, in the 1920s and 1930s, he was exposed to Marxism, and well into his career he held distinct views on the relation of art to labor, convictions which were at the heart of his approach to his art. In this and other ways, he connected to an old American tradition of artists who are deeply committed to political and social causes, and who consider their art an expression of their commitment, although it is not immediately apparent.

As a person, Porter could be as abrupt as his art seemed. He would enter a room without notice, engage an acquaintance directly, without preliminaries or niceties, make his point, and depart suddenly, without leave.[6] He was anything but a picture of perceived WASP affability. He could also be contrary in his views, and certainly in his art, a quality which in part explains his refusal to paint abstractly. He was sometimes content to show lesser or even failed pictures, perhaps knowing that the standards on which these judgments were made might well change, but also because he was not afraid to test usual standards of quality and finish. The vitality in a painting was far more important to him than its finish.

Porter was anything but detached in his work and in his aesthetic judgment. His art depended on a distinct, variant reading of modernism, which gives us cause to reconsider our own views of this history. Indeed, he was one—or perhaps even the only—practicing artist of his generation who was also a true intellectual. He read extensively. He wrote poetry. He thought about his art and about both past and current art in a considered and thorough manner. He lectured and he taught. He had begun to write in the 1930s. From 1951 until 1961 he wrote steadily, contributing monthly reviews to *Art News* and *The Nation*. Thereafter he wrote longer, more general pieces.[7] It is no coincidence that Porter's painting reached its first full maturity in 1951, just when he began to write. His writing made him a better painter, and his painting made him a better writer. Porter had more confidence in his writing than he did in his painting, but he became both a fine painter and one of the most lucid and intelligent art critics and writers of the post-1945 period. His insights are unique, and the range of his taste is surprising and intriguing. His work should be read by anyone who is seriously interested in modern art.

A S AN ARTIST, Porter is now a far more familiar figure than he once was, but it is worth examining his life if we are to understand his art.[8] He was born in 1907, which placed him in the same generation as the Abstract Expressionists; de Kooning and Gorky were born in 1904, Kline in 1910, and Pollock in 1912. Porter's circumstances, of course, were far different. He was born into a large and affluent family in the prosperous Chicago suburb of Winnetka, Illinois (then known as Hubbard Woods). His parents were educated and cultured; his father was an architect who designed the family houses, first in Winnetka and later in Maine. There, the family acquired Great Spruce Head Island in Penobscot Bay in 1912. From that time on, Porter spent virtually every summer of his life there, and the island became more his home than any other place.

The senior Porter did not practice architecture to any extent, and spent most of his time looking after the family's real estate interests. Fairfield's mother's family had owned farmland which eventually had become the Loop in downtown Chicago, and it was this which accounted for the family fortune. His father introduced a knowledge of the natural sciences, architecture, and certainly of the visual arts, for the house was filled with reproductions of old master paintings. Porter's mother, too, was college-educated, a phenomenon that was still a rarity at the turn of the century, and she read incessantly, especially in classical literature. She took Fairfield to The Art Institute of Chicago, when he was at an early age. When he was fifteen the family went to Europe, the first of many trips, where he saw paintings by Leonardo, Titian, and Veronese. From early childhood, Porter drew, and he was good at it; he copied drawings by Howard Pyle as well as making copies from photographs. Just before he entered Harvard, he took a few private lessons.

How vastly different Porter's background was from that of his peers, most of whom had suffered poverty and deprivation to one degree or another! Nevertheless, he did not emerge unscathed from his privileged upbringing. None of us does, and all the affluence in the world could not protect him from certain vulnerabilities. The young Fairfield was shy and isolated in high school, in part because he was two years younger than his classmates. His family was demanding, and it had strong, perhaps even impossibly lofty ideas about what its children should be and should do. In later life Porter remembered the difficulty that came from "being told as a child (and I seem not to have got rid of this yet) that I, Fairfield, am the way someone else has decided I am."[9] In fact, Porter apparently had been robbed of his identity at the age of three, when his parents took away his original name and gave it to his younger brother, John.[10] Later, his father doubted that he had the requisite talent to be an artist.[11] It is small wonder that Porter suffered a lack of a real sense of self-esteem. Throughout his life, he was beset with crises of confidence about himself and about his painting. Certainly his lack of self-confidence was an important factor in his slow development as a painter.

Porter was seventeen when he entered Harvard in 1924. There he became deeply interested in the Fine Arts. He took Arthur Pope's famous course in "Drawing and Painting and Principles of Design," became acquainted with Berenson's ideas of aesthetics, and studied philosophy with Alfred North Whitehead, who was to become an important influence for him. Whitehead taught him the importance of being specific, for escaping vagueness, for defining his terms and his position.[12] Since no studio courses were offered, the emphasis in the arts at Harvard was on theory, and primary concentration was on the old masters (although Pope was interested in modern art). When Porter graduated in 1928, he listed his future profession as "Painting."[13]

That fall of 1928 Porter moved to New York and enrolled at The Art Students League. He studied there for two years with Thomas Hart Benton and Boardman Robinson. He thought Robinson a better teacher because he taught the students as individuals; Benton had a rigid system, one of "bumps and hollows" that denied, in Porter's mind, the real and sensuous qualities of painting.[14] A few figure paintings in the Benton style remain, which demonstrate why Porter believed that no one at the League, and probably no one in America, really knew how to paint. He resolved that he would have to teach himself.[15] He was virtually a beginner, and thus he embarked on a long and trying apprenticeship that would last for twenty years before his first mature, distinctive art emerged. This alone should warn us that what looks casual and off-hand in Porter's art was in fact hard won.

Little work remains from this early period. In 1931-1932, Porter traveled widely in Europe, and lived in Italy. There he continued to study and to make copies of old master paintings, almost as if he were continuing his Harvard education, rather than plunging into the past and current developments of modern art. This no doubt delayed him, but in the end the instinct to maintain the fullness and wholeness of the old masters became a strength of his work, and exemplified the fact that artists have always sought guidance and help in older art. In his later life Cézanne went to the Louvre to see if he had painted as well as he hoped. In 1907, Matisse journeyed to Italy to study Giotto, seeking something more permanent and stable for his own art. The American modernists Morton Schamberg and Charles Sheeler admired Piero della Francesca's firm line, which became the basis of their mature art. Such practice and emulation is not, as Rackstraw Downes has pointed out, a reactionary path. It is a more ambitious course, for it enables the artist to build on and expand the means available to him.[16] In so far as it always strives to maintain the best qualities of past art, painting, even modern painting, is a conservative activity in the literal sense of the word.

From all accounts, Porter was an eager and enthusiastic student in these years.[17] But this enthusiasm did not translate itself into his art until 1949-1951. The question remains as to why. We have noted the matter of his self-confidence, which was very real. But other currents were at work as well. In 1927, while he was in Europe, Porter had visited Russia and had become in sympathy with Marx and socialism. The social and economic turmoil of the 1930s drew him increasingly into identifying with the radical politics of the time once he returned to America in 1932. He painted murals "more or less in imitation of Orozco"[18] and the Mexicans; he wrote for the socialist magazine *Arise*, he produced illustrations for poetry magazines and engaged in the causes and the political discourse of the day. All probably distracted him from giving his full and undivided attention to painting.

With a private income, Porter never had to work, except for a period in the early forties. At a time of extreme poverty in America, which affected his fellow artists even more deeply than might otherwise have been the case, his affluence surely caused him guilt, which hindered his progress. His sympathy for socialism and the proletariat made it difficult for him to regard painting as a valuable labor, and his struggle to secure this sense of worth for his art was exacerbated by world economic conditions. His financial independence also isolated him from a sense of community with other artists because his income disqualified him from joining the WPA, one of the common experiences for American artists shared during the 1930s.

In addition, there were family concerns. Porter had married the poet Anne Channing in 1932, and by 1936 they had two children. John, the oldest, some years later was discovered to be retarded and was taken to a foster home to live. But at first his condition was not diagnosed, and a difficult burden was placed on the young family. The anguish and turmoil caused Porter to believe he had somehow failed as a father. Later, he wrote a friend that the situation with John had distracted him to the extent that he had been unable to make a life or career for himself until they had found John a home where he could be properly cared for.[19]

In 1936, searching for a suitable place to live for his family, Porter moved back to Winnetka into the old family house. This further isolated him, although in 1937 he wrote that "I keep on learning about oil painting. It is the most difficult medium..."[20] Such notes confirm that Porter was not a natural painter, that he had to teach himself through sheer perseverance. Because it was the "most difficult medium," it would take a long time before he would paint successfully in oil. But if the process was slow, this, too, had its rewards. If he was isolated, he was also free from the pressures of aesthetic dogma that plagued the 1930s, just as it plagues the 1990s. Porter could be open to pursue his own instincts and his own views of the history of art. And he could do it at his own pace.

In 1938-1939, two decisive events occurred. The first was an exhibition of the works of Bonnard and Vuillard, which Porter saw at The Art Institute of Chicago late in 1938. Later he would observe that at first he thought the Vuillards were perhaps "just a revelation of the obvious," but then again, he understood "why did one think of doing anything else when it was so natural to do that." What he liked in Vuillard, he said, was that "what he's doing seems ordinary, but the extraordinary is everywhere."[21] After his struggles with socialist theories about the only permissable content of art, with family concerns, and with his now ten years of teaching himself to paint, how tonic and how sure the private, painterly world of Bonnard and Vuillard must have seemed! These artists gave Porter a grounding and direction he had sorely lacked in his work. They provided a way that would free him, once and for all, from the ideological debates of the thirties. Their message was clear: paint what you know, what is given to you, what is in front of you, and let the painting speak for itself. Because their work of the Nabi period is best known, we tend to think of Bonnard and Vuillard as late nineteenth-century artists, and in a sense they are. But in the late 1930s both were still living masters. They offered Porter a way to see the continuity of modern art, from its roots in the nineteenth century to the present. They mediated between past and present, offering Porter a way to translate the solid, durable world of old master art into a vital and personal modern art.

In his art criticism, Porter noted aspects of Vuillard's art, especially the late work which we can now see had important parallels in his own work. (It is interesting to note that Porter's writings on other artists often contain essential points to be made about his own art.) For example, on the occasion of Vuillard's retrospective at The Museum of Modern Art in New York in 1954, Porter wrote that it was actually Vuillard who had accomplished Cézanne's wish to make something solid and enduring of Impressionism, like the art of the museums.[22] Porter believed that Vuillard had succeeded in unifying "the Impressionist shimmer into a single object, instead of like Cézanne denying the essence of the shimmer by changing it into planes to express solidity." In Vuillard, Porter found an artist in whom, "the Idea is the absence of an Idea," an essential tenet of Porter's own art. Porter's grasp of this was surely a reaction to the rhetoric of the thirties. For him, Vuillard's art was "concrete in detail and abstract as a whole," a quality which was "just the opposite of Cubism." Porter believed that Cubism had made art into something too intellectual, that it had been particularly harmful to American painters because it got them away from what they knew, from their own experience. For him, the famous Armory Show of 1913 was a disaster because it was the event most responsible for provoking this turn. Vuillard was crucial in helping Porter to get past ideologies, to trust his own instincts, and to give way to the sensuous qualities of painting.

Porter admired Vuillard's ability to "put together everything before him," and praised him for the talent "to construct that surpasses the abstract painters." He found that Vuillard had a "sensitiveness that is more personal than that of the Impressionists, and therefore more human." Porter revealed something important about himself in 1954 when he said of Vuillard: "He is thought of as soft and private. Privacy is also the essence of bourgeois life in France."[23]

Bonnard, too, was important for him. He admired Bonnard's spatial organization, which did not "repeat the consistency of actuality—the woman in front melts into recession, a shadow or the sky is palpable."[24] Like Porter, Bonnard was an "intellectual but had no Idea." He was, for Porter, "an individualist without revolt, and his form, which is more complete and thorough than any abstract painter's, comes from his tenderness."[25]

In 1939, after Porter had moved back to the East, he met Willem de Kooning. This, too, was a decisive event. Porter later confirmed that he had learned more about painting from de Kooning than from anyone else.[26] As was the case with Vuillard's influence, the full impact de Kooning had on Porter was not apparent in his work until after 1950. Then, de Kooning's bold, fluent use of paint gave Porter a means to transform the intimate world of Vuillard and Bonnard into his own distinctive painterly expression.

Nevertheless, de Kooning's example may already have been evident, if only distantly, in Porter's *Seated Boy* (fig. 1) of the late 1930s. The muted palette refers the painting to thirties realism; it also suggests an awareness of Velázquez, whom Berenson had recommended to Porter in 1932 as perhaps the greatest painter of all. But the solemn figure of the painting may be based, too, in the paintings of men that de Kooning was producing in the late thirties and early forties.

Porter and de Kooning seem worlds apart, and in ways they are, but they to a surprising degree also shared common attitudes. Both had been trained in the old masters. De Kooning, Dutch by birth, had his roots in the grand European tradition of old master painting. Before he came to America in 1926, he had been trained in the art of the past at the Academy in Rotterdam. In the early 1930s, de Kooning painted fine abstractions, but by 1935 he had begun to paint figuratively, which he continued to do throughout his career. He was, as Stephen Polcari has noted, the figure painter of Abstract Expressionism, just as Renoir was the traditional figure painter of Impressionism.[27] Thus de Kooning was the most conservative—in the literal sense of the word—painter of the Abstract Expressionist group. This was one of the links Porter must have felt with de Kooning. Both also clearly wished to retain something of the old tradition while seeking a new and contemporary language. In the years from c. 1939-1944 de Kooning (and Gorky) particularly admired Ingres, as is evident in the strong linearity of their figures. The precise rendering of the folds in Porter's *Seated Boy* may also reflect an interest in Ingres.

For Porter at the time, it may well be that de Kooning alone offered the example of a fresh and authentic figurative painting. This would have been welcome, and revelatory, given the sorry state of most Depression-era figurative painting. It was, after all, his failure to find mentors for this type of painting which had caused Porter in the first place to teach himself to paint. In 1942 (according to Porter's later recall; the date is uncertain), Clement Greenberg told de Kooning that it was impossible to paint the figure any longer.[28] De Kooning replied that it was impossible not to paint the figure. Porter remembered that he resolved then and there to paint the figure, to do precisely what was said couldn't be done. He added that he might have painted abstractly had it not been for this encounter. This is doubtful; abstraction was never in Porter's experience; he had been rooted in the art of the old masters from his boyhood. Further, as Hilton Kramer, an early and forceful champion of Porter, has pointed out, Porter was too intelligent and thoughtful to base his art on a single, chance encounter of this sort.[29] But Porter's statement does highlight the kinship between Porter and de Kooning for the possibilities of the figure. Like Porter, de Kooning had a contrary streak. Not only did he switch to figuration in the late thirties, when others were moving to abstraction, but he also chose to explore Depression grimness just as the era was closing. This is a realist point of view; here and later, de Kooning, as did Porter, wished to merge glimpses of the known world with the old master figurative tradition.

As we have observed, the lessons of de Kooning, as well as those of Bonnard and Vuillard, were slow to germinate. Extant Porter paintings from the mid- and late 1940s are few. Those that survive are primarily urban scenes—Porter was living in New York City—and still rooted in the ideology of the 1930s. However, in *Cityscape* (fig. 2) of c. 1945, there is a strong light which was distinctly Porter's own. In another association with light, around 1945, Porter—still the student—was copying a Tiepolo in The Metropolitan Museum of Art when a refugee Belgian painter named Van Houten came up and observed him at work. He told Porter that he had light in his paintings, and that this was rare. (Who better than Tiepolo to look at to learn about light?) Porter got to know Van Houten and took a few lessons from him. Van Houten urged him to keep on seeing light in everything, even in the shadows, and above all, to see light in pigment rather than paint. This advice, Porter remembered, was important; it was something he knew, but it was something he needed to hear at this time from someone else. The advice stayed with him, and Porter's mature art was permeated by light, myriad kinds of light.[30]

In 1945, Porter took a course with Jacques Maroger at the Parsons School of Design, which gave him another needed push. Maroger taught him to use what he called "The Medium," a mixture of beeswax, lead carbonate, and raw linseed oil which is boiled until it is pitch black. It can be mixed with the oils, or used to prime the canvas. When mixed with the medium, paints remain fluid and flexible. They can be worked with or changed with ease and rapidity. Maroger's medium gave Porter a fluency, an ease, and a new confidence that he had been lacking. From this he developed a fuller awareness of the nature of paint, of its physical properties, of its sensuousness and full-bodied qualities.[31]

Just after the war, Porter saw the Velásquez infantas paintings from the Kaiser Friedrich Museum in a loan exhibition at the Metropolitan. He had seen them on a visit to Berlin, but he now was taken by them anew. With his new interest in the nature of paint and what one can do with it, Porter admired the "liquid surface" of Velásquez, and his understatement. "He leaves things alone. It isn't that he copies nature; he doesn't impose himself on it. He is open to it, rather than wanting to twist it. Let the paint dictate to you." Porter's regard for the natural quality in Velásquez, for "the paint," is what characterizes his mature art, done after 1950.[32] It was a search for a seamless, interwoven surface, in which the order is as it is given, as one finds it, without rearranging it.

Porter moved his large and growing family to Southampton in October 1949. It is precisely at this time that he made his first distinctive art. It may also be that de Kooning's exhibition in 1948, his first one-man show, may have been an inspiration. But apparently the move from the city, away from urban spaces to an open and green landscape, permeated by light, had a salutary effect on his work. His writing, which he began doing on a regular basis in 1951 for *Art News*, also was important. His monthly reviews brought him into contact with the larger community of practicing and exhibiting artists with an intensity he had not experienced before. It required him to look hard at all manner of artists. The process forced him to consider and define his own art with a new clarity, and there is no doubt it hastened the emergence of his painting.

Even then, with the move to Southampton, Porter's paintings of 1949-1951 were interior scenes and portraits rather than landscapes. He chose to paint what was immediately around him, as for example, *Painting Materials* (fig. 5), c. 1949, and *Studio Interior* (fig. 6) of 1951. These paintings remind us how he had gone about the task of learning to paint: "So I just set about copying the way things looked and trying to get it down ... It doesn't matter much what you do. What matters is the painting. And since a reference to reality is the easiest thing you just take what's there. And then you hope it's significant."[33] But it does matter what you paint, of course, and these paintings are significant for what they depict. They are, in the words Porter used to describe the art of painting, "dense with experience." The phrase is telling; Porter borrowed it from John Szarkowski, who used it to describe the work of Atget, whom Porter, too, considered a great artist.[34] The words capture the place, and the means, of the struggle Porter had undertaken more than twenty years earlier to become, now finally, an accomplished painter. Porter is never sentimental or adventitious. But here, as elsewhere, he painted his biography, just as he understood that he was painting his father's biography when he painted the house his father had built in Maine.

These early pictures are unassuming, or even reticent at first. Unadorned, and with little color, they are in the low-key, realist tradition not only of Velásquez, but of Chardin, Corot, and Courbet, artists whom Porter also admired. We can say they represent his first way of making a "natural" type of picture. There is the sure, firm handling, and each element has a distinct place, with a specific weight and density. With time—which is Porter's way—further complexities and subtleties of the art of painting reveal themselves in these apparently simple pictures. For example, in *Painting Materials*, the radical tilt forecasts his predilection for novel, unexpected viewing angles in his paintings. The strong and open brushing, which fills out and activates the whole surface, indicates that de Kooning's brush had now set an important example for Porter. In *Studio Interior*, the easel, and especially the stove, take on an anthropomorphic presence, for Porter believed objects have a life of their own. The painting on the easel, a painting within a painting, also forecasts another recurring theme. Besides being a painting, it is both a mirror and a window, for it seems to both continue the center line, as if we were looking through it, and to reflect the whole of the composition as well. The painting itself is laid out like an interior still life, and the way the objects connect demonstrates Porter's continuing concern for the "relatedness" of things. We here first witness that when Porter painted, he tried not to see the object as it was, but "to see only concrete shapes which have no association except as themselves,"—to see only where one thing ends and another begins.[35]

By 1952, Porter had introduced more color in paintings, as in *Laurence Typing* (fig. 7), an interior scene recalling Vuillard and Bonnard. He was helped in his use of color by the example of the artists around him, especially Jane Freilicher.[36] A new confidence is evident in the broader and more complex range of placements, textures, surfaces, and space. The figure is but one object among many, part of a series of major and minor chords of diagonals created by the furniture and books. In turn, these are opposed in Porter's architecture of the space by the vertical rectangles of the mirror and windows. Porter's work is permeated by light, which has been frequently noted. But it should also be noted that he mastered many types of light, interior and exterior, natural and artificial. Here he undertakes a particularly difficult problem: conveying interior artificial light and simultaneously, reflected light in the mirror.

In his handling of these types of light, Porter ranks with Vuillard and Edward Hopper. The use of mirrors and windows as reflectors of people, objects, architecture, and space itself were another pictorial element that Porter used daringly throughout his work. They are one more element that causes us to question using realism as a gauge of Porter's art; because he disdained bravura and theatrical handling, his complexity disguises itself. Now, with a new level of accomplishment, Porter's art came to the attention of the public in 1952 with his first one-man show, held at the Tibor de Nagy Gallery. Fittingly enough, it had come about through the recommendation of de Kooning.

Porter returned to landscape in a sustained manner in 1952-1954. Once more he painted his familiar, immediate surroundings, his yard in Southampton, and views of the woods and ocean in Maine. In the presence of the broad and open reaches of the land and sea around him, he opened up with a new expansiveness in his painting. He seems now to trust more in his instincts, to let the brush take over, to allow the real and physical qualities of paint dictate his course. In the Southampton landscapes, Porter activated a rough, vigorous surface that was the equivalent of Abstract Expressionist paint handling. Indeed, Porter was more at home with the Abstract Expressionists than he was with those who termed themselves realists. Porter does not use contour lines, but draws and shapes with the paint. For Porter, one of the discoveries of Impressionism was that contour was unimportant relative to the interior light, substance, and weight of what it contained.[37] The physicality of the paint is evident; air and space are on the same plane and have the same weight as the trees. Porter found another type of landscape at the same time, which he painted mostly along the trails and paths of the island in Maine. In contrast to the open format, these "trail" pictures are smaller and more compact, with a close focus on a small area of woods, grass, or flowers. They show us just what Porter meant when he insisted that he painted what he saw, rather than what he might assume to be there. It is the particularity of each object and each site that he observes and records. They speak tellingly of his insistence on the specific, concrete facts of painting. Despite—or because of—the small format, Porter could achieve a large and expansive internal scale, and he was often especially successful with the small format. These paintings form a sub-category of Porter's landscape work, though they have been hardly noticed.

Porter was a late starter, but once under way, he never looked

back. It is a fact of his career that after 1950 he continued to improve, and he was painting his very best pictures at the end of his life. His skill and range grew dramatically in the years from 1955 to 1958. It is at this time that he consistently does major paintings. *Armchair on Porch* (fig. 11), painted in 1955 at the house in Maine, is a masterful study of low-keyed light, reminding us of Van Houten's dictum to paint light even in the shadows. It demonstrates just how arbitary Porter's painting can be. The focal point is pushed, as it often is, off center, to an unexpected spot, here in the upper right. This angle empties much of the painting, and we are given in the center a surface of pure painting alive and filled with rippling light and shadow, which becomes the true subject. Rackstraw Downes was surely right when he observed that "there is no subject in Porter's painting until he starts working on it" (see note 45). Porter himself remarked that the artist who searches for subject matter is like the person who can't get out of bed without understanding the meaning of life. As he had noted of Bonnard, he did not "repeat the consistency of actuality." The light is in and of the floor, it becomes impossible to distinguish it from the concrete floor itself. This feel of immateriality extends even to the chair, which is almost transparent. The vertical screen frame has virtually disappeared so that the distant sky merges with and becomes as palpable as the shadows and patterns of light on the floor. The transparency of the picture is Whistlerian, braced only by the structuring of the screens and patterns of light. Porter loved to paint from and on the porches of the house in Maine, precisely for these reasons.

The pitch of color and light was thereafter considerably heightened in paintings such as the 1955 *Katie and Anne* (fig. 12). Light engulfs the room and the two figures, who in their frailness suggest the figures of Corot. Here, the areas of the sofa connecting Anne with the chair, and the shadows on the curtains, are transformed into independent, abstract patterns of shape and color, of palpable paint. It reminds us of Porter's admiration for the way Vuillard "put together everything before him."[38] The surface is as a single entity, all of it simultaneously present. Porter sought, as did Matisse, to make every corner of the canvas alive. This painting should be considered a companion piece to the 1958 *Anne, Lizzie and Katie* (fig. 17), with the family seen on the other side of the same room, and to the great *Portait of Elaine de Kooning* (fig. 14), done in 1957. We should note here that in a review of 1960, Porter described the work of Alex Katz in terms that equally apply to his own art: "Alex Katz is a 'realist,' meaning you recognize every detail in his paintings, and the whole too, though the whole takes precedence and the detail may be only an area of color, in short, abstract."[39]

De Kooning's example of bold, direct paint application continued to serve Porter in the two still lifes (figs. 15 and 16) of 1958. Flowers, walls, windows, and space itself are brushed so that all textures have the same density and painterly weight. The backgrounds have greater prominence, and appear closer to us than what we would assume to be closer to us. Here, paint is as real as nature, as Porter termed it. Writing about de Kooning in 1959, Porter noted, as he might have of his own pictures: "The colors are intense—not 'bright,' not 'primary'—but intensely themselves, as if each color has been freed to be. The few large strokes ... also have this freed quality."[40] Porter's areas and strokes here distinctly call to mind de Kooning's landscape abstractions of 1957-1959. They also recall Porter's description of Katz's work: "The colors and shapes which are necessary expressions of each other, make, without losing any part of their individuality, even in the flattest simplification, an integral space, the manifestation of an integral spiritual whole."[41]

In the 1960s, Porter began to paint with a new sweep and broadness. In the landscapes, for example, areas might be fewer, but they tended to be larger and more expansive, as was apparent as early as the 1961 sea view, *Calm Morning* (fig. 21). He was seeking, as he later said, to retain the spontaneity of Impressionism, but he also wanted something "large and deliberate."[42] Drawing and shaping became increasingly arbitrary and abstract, as well as more fluent and subtle. The size of his pictures increased, and by 1965 he was regularly making paintings that were five, six, or seven feet on a side. These tendencies reflected, in part, a general shift after 1957 toward greater clarity and stability by both Abstract Expressionists and younger artists of the post-painterly generation.

Porter considerably broadened the vistas of his landscapes in paintings such as the 1963 *Short Walk* (fig. 24), his *Six O'Clock* (fig. 27) of 1964, and the 1965 *Morning Landscape* (fig. 30) , all remarkable pictures. We may ask, again, what is the subject? Human incident is secondary, and we come across it almost as if by surprise. The life of the paintings is in the proliferation of shapes and patterns, of areas of paint and color whose sheer inventiveness and sense of ceaseless, organic growth could be rivaled only by the abstractions of Clyfford Still. They tell us just how Porter acted on his belief that effective composition was not the repetition of elements, as he had been taught at Harvard. It was just the opposite: that nothing was repeated, and "If there's something that never occurs again in a painting that's what is its unique quality."[43] Each of these three landscapes has a different type of light and coloring, the first autumnal, the second almost surreal in its verdant depths, and the third, *Morning Landscape*, filled with pearlescent colors of first light, as if we are in a new world. This painting is framed by the architecture of the porch screen, almost as if it were a painting within a painting, another variant of a Porter motif. With its view of a figure placed against the Maine woods and the ocean (another favorite motif), it is a miracle of freshness and invention. On its seamless, single surface, inside and outside, weight and transparency, light and shadow, air and water, the human and the natural are simultaneously presented as facts of painting. For it was not expressionism that interested Porter, but the "visualness" of things. He spoke of how he wanted to look out and see the environment as if for the first time; what interested him was the first experience, the idea that "The world starts in this picture."[44]

The paintings look effortless, but this quality is the essence of the natural picture. The approach by now was a hard-won, effective working method for Porter. He paints "without fuss," as Rackstraw Downes put it.[45] Louis Finkelstein defined this work as a formal re-sponse to the "strained" quality of modernism.[46] It is, he said, a self-aware attitude, that conceals its artfulness and intelligence by a display of nonchalance. It is discreet, and avoids the appearance of virtuosity. The subject matter is normal, and commonplace, and it is rendered without elaborate composition or sumptuous technique.

In the 1960s, interior scenes with one or several figures also accounted for some of Porter's best paintings. The 1964 *The Screen Porch* (fig. 25) included four figures on the back porch in Maine, fusing an interior and outdoor space. The figures are large and general, like Giotto's, but they convey little apparent emotion. *July Interior* (fig. 26) of 1964 depicts Anne sick in bed; she is seen from a vantage point that is level with the bed, a particularly unexpected perspective. The picture is filled with commonplace objects, and no special effort has been made to order them. Porter painted interiors and still lifes as he found them, because for him, this was the reality of our experience: "What you are is simply what you've been saying all this time."[47] But into this mundane array, Porter infuses a ceaseless activity, the special and innate vitality of a painted surface.

Novel perspectives that rival Velásquez are seen in *The Mirror* (fig. 32), surely one of Porter's most remarkable paintings. The sitter and mirror confront us, and the mirror is structured as a painting within a painting, one rectangle within another, as clear as a non-objective painting. But the mirror then opens up to a deep vista that includes the artist and a view through to the house. Although diverse and diffused, all this is presented as part of our immediate, known experience. We can understand why Porter said that painting is not driven more by the intellectual or the emotional, but "is a way of making the connection between yourself and everything."[48] For him, what is real is specific and total. Art is not an ideal, but is material and actual.

The Mirror was the first of a series of self-portraits, produced in the studio, and portraits of family, done sometimes, but not always, in the studio, that Porter painted in the late 1960s. Porter also used reflected outdoor vistas to similar effect in the 1960s and 1970s, as in the 1971 *Portrait of a Girl* (fig. 50), in which the distant ocean is seen in the window behind the seated figure. In these paintings we see him arriving at the height of his powers. Their complexity as well as their richness should put to rest any remaining thoughts that Porter's art is either easy or casual. When we compare the two portraits of Anne (figs. 31 and 37), which were painted within two years of each other, we can see the great range Porter had achieved. In the first, from 1965, Anne is seated on the porch. The portrait is suffused with a quiet, reflective mood that borders on the austere. Certainly, it could be termed a "slow" picture. But the more we study the painting, the more insistent and the more complex it becomes. The articulation of the structure of the floor and the wall, and how they are joined and made to relate to the seated figure, are masterful passages of the art of painting. The wall is as clear and straightforward as a minimalist painting of the sixties; add to this the complexities within the play of color, with its narrow and rich spectrum of Whistlerian grays, whites, and blues, and we have a painting of quite another order. Porter had a singular touch with the myriad tones of gray, a hue we do not really consider when we discuss color. Porter's niece, Anina Porter Fuller, herself an accomplished artist, was doubtless right when she observed that gray was Porter's signature color.[49] As a companion piece to this first 1960s portrait, we might consider a later painting, the 1974 *Anne in Doorway* (fig. 63), in which these grays are now enriched and contrasted by a deep wine red in the background, a sequence that demonstrates just how good a colorist Porter became.

The second 1960s portrait, *Anne in a Striped Dress* (fig. 37), also contains passages of gray, but it is a much different type of painting, as are the self-portraits done in the studio. This is a more immediate painting, more complex and active than the seated Anne. But it, too, yields only slowly the full depth of its complexities, found in the sudden, unexplained shifts of space, color, and shaping between and within the several parts of the composition. Here Anne stands on the second floor of the studio-barn in Southampton; we look out past her to the house, in a view that seems as if it could only have been painted from the first floor. Any sense of middle or deep space is negated, and the house appears as being as close to the viewer as the wall. The large window and the background it frames become another wall, which acts as if it, too, were a painting within a painting. The repetition of shapes echoes the several rectangles of the reproductions on the wall to the right of Anne. In turn, the window responds to the windows of the house at the rear, setting up a sequence of geometries across the surface. These rectangles are in turn contrasted and activated by the intertwining drawing of the tree branches. All this is tied together in a single, concrete interlocking surface. The formality, and the detail, remind us of the tension between realism and abstraction in Porter's art, and we remember Porter's warning that "The realist thinks he knows ahead of time what reality is, and the abstract artist what art is, but it is in its formality that realist art excels, and the best abstract art communicates an overwhelming sense of reality."[50] Just how he pulls together this diverse painterly array into a resonant, harmonious whole is at the heart of his accomplishment.

In Porter's depiction of house, studio, and family, this and the other studio paintings contain a powerful biography. This extends to Anne's dress and the brilliant red Shaker robe on the stool next to her, for these were family treasures passed down from her mother. Porter's political and painterly interests are evident in the photographs on the wall, which include a reproduction of a Velásquez and an old *Life* magazine cover of Adlai Stevenson, both of whom he deeply admired. Truly, these paintings are "dense with experience."

The landscapes Porter did in the last years of his life, his culminating works, also show the range that this slow-starting, self-taught artist had reached. In the late sixties, in *Amherst Campus No. 1* (fig. 45) and *Island Farmhouse* (fig.44), he introduced a particular flat, crisp kind of color that could be almost Fauve in its intensity. It is the pervasive, intense light that is truly compelling in these late paintings. The light may be soft and diffused, or sharp and clear, as in the 1973 *Sunrise on South Main Street* (fig. 59) Porter could be at home with types of light as different as those found in the fluency of the two great snow pictures of c. 1972 (figs. 53 and 54) or in the blue and gray staccato rhythms of beach and waves in the 1972 *Ocean*. (fig. 56) The vista could be wide, opening out on the expanses of shore and harbor in the 1974 paintings *The Dock* (fig. 60) and *The Harbor—Great Spruce Head* (fig. 61), two works which show how Porter could vary the same scene. Or the painting could be enclosed and private, venturing no further than the Porter back yard in Southampton, as in *The Privet Hedge* (fig. 65), done only months before his death in 1975. The scene might be taken as the very essence of Porter. It was part of his daily existence, so common as hardly to constitute a subject. There is only a house, a hedge, and the family dog. But in Porter, in the ordinary there is the extraordinary. The painting is filled with authenticity and truth and it is complex; it is a frontal view, divided into three zones, something like a Rothko. In the hedge there is a richness of organic pattern, of pure painting that is as powerful and direct as a Still, a late Pollock, and even the oils of John Marin, whom he had long ago admired. It shows us how Porter was far more interested in how things connect and relate, than in their exact look. It is an art of touch and of nuance, rich with feeling and a lifetime of experience. He had always taken American painting to task for its dim, puritanical light, and in these late works, it is as if he had taken it upon himself to claim for American painting the same full, high-keyed light that is one of the glories of French Impressionist art.

Although his early training was formed in Europe, Porter was a distinctly American artist. There was, first, his understanding of the American past. He believed that no one here really knew how to paint, and that he would have to teach himself, just as American artists had to do in the past. Then there was the struggle to justify and accept painting as real work. He saw this struggle in Eakins, about whom he had written, and with whom he identified, since Eakins, too, had been independently wealthy. Porter admired de Kooning in part because he solved this problem, seeing the art in honest labor, and vice versa.

There was the directness of Porter's attack on the canvas, the belief in the life of the paint, and the abruptness within given passages. In his search, Porter was willing to allow and to admit to his mistakes, and was content to retain and exhibit the record of his struggle with the medium. He did not feel the need to hide the bluntness of his pictures under painterly guises, a quality that is in line with a long American tradition. Porter is distinctly American because of his insistence on the concrete and the specific rather than on the European heritage of the ideal and the general. He worked empirically, an approach deeply rooted in the American experience. In other ways, he stands with an American tradition of artists who are deeply committed to political and social views, but who let them speak metaphorically through the painterly, abstract qualities of their art.

Above all, Porter should be seen in the tradition of American individualism. In his insistence on the real and concrete nature of experience, on the distinctness and diversity, even the arbitrary nature, of facts, Porter proclaimed the triumph of the individual. It was a triumph of the individual over technocracy and the state, of the singular over the general, of the real and vital over the standardized and the routine, of the natural over the artificial. These ideas were profound, and critical for him, for he had experienced Russia and socialism at first hand, and had matured during the 1930s when the very existence of these values was threatened.

In Porter's view, art does not stand for anything outside itself. Art is measured by its interior intensity and its capacity to compel our imagination. Paint is as real as nature, and the means of painting can contain its ends. At its fullest, art lays bare the soul of the artist. Sadly, these ideas do not have much currency today, at a time when our society has suffered a pervasive loss of affirmation. But they are valuable, and worth heeding. The sheer accomplishment of Porter's art, which needs no explanation or justification, is eloquent testimony to their value. Should we need further evidence of their importance, Porter himself might have supplied the answer in his review of the 1959 de Kooning show. He might well have been speaking of himself and his own art when he wrote: " ... everything is at its own limits of possibilities. What does this do to the person who looks at the paintings? This: the picture presented of released possibilities, of ordinary qualities existing at their fullest limits and acting harmoniously together—this picture is exalting."[51]

WILLIAM C. AGEE
Professor of Art, Hunter College

NOTES

1 Most notably in the title of the catalogue of the important exhibition organized by Kenworth Moffett in 1982 for the Museum of Fine Arts, Boston, *Fairfield Porter/Realist Painter in an Age of Abstraction*. The catalogue is crucial for the study of Porter. Hereafter referred to as Moffett.

2 "The Human Figure Returns in Separate Ways and Places," *Life*, 52, 23; June 8, 1962; p. 57.

3 This was developed by Louis Finkelstein, "The Naturalness of Fairfield Porter," *Arts Magazine*, 50, 9; May 1976: pp. 102-105; and by Robert Berlind, "Fairfield Porter: Natural Premises," *Art in America*, 71, 8; Sept. 1983; pp. 136-143.

4 As reported by Trudy C. Kramer to the author, Fall, 1991.

5 Paul Cummings, interview with Fairfield Porter, June 6, 1968: p. 72. Archives of American Art, Smithsonian Institution, Washington, D.C., and New York. Hereafter referred to as Cummings.

6 See John Bernard Myers, "Jottings from a Diary (1952-1975)," in Moffett, pp. 41, 43.

7 An extensive selection of Porter's art writing has been gathered and edited by Rackstraw Downes, with an excellent introduction, in *Art in Its Own Terms/ Selected Criticism 1953-1975*. Cambridge, Mass.: Zoland, 1993; reprint of 1979 Taplinger edition. Hereafter referred to as Downes.

8 There is now a full biography by John T. Spike, *Fairfield Porter/An American Classic*. New York: Abrams, 1992. Hereafter referred to as Spike.

9 Porter letter to Claire White, courtesy of Ted Leigh, a former student of Porter's who is gathering the letters. The manuscript is hereafter referred to as Leigh.

10 Leigh.

11 Spike, p. 21, interview with Eliot Porter.

12 Cummings, pp. 16-18.

13 Harvard Yearbook, 1928.

14 Cummings, pp. 20-22.

15 Ibid.

16 Rackstraw Downes, "What the Sixties Meant to Me," *Art Journal*, 34, 2; Winter 1974/75: pp. 125-131.

17 See Spike and Moffett.

18 Cummings, pp. 20-23.

19 Letter to Arthur Giardelli, January, 1958; quoted in Moffett, p. 24.

20 Spike, p. 20.

21 Cummings.

22 Fairfield Porter, "Vuillard," 1954, in Downes, p. 170.

23 Ibid.

24 "Bonnard, 1956." Ibid., pp. 171-172.

25 Ibid.

26 Cummings, p. 51.

27 Stephen Polcari, *Abstract Expressionism and The Modern Experience*. New York: Cambridge University Press, 1991: pp. 263-274.

28 In a 1962 essay Porter gave the date as 1942. See Downes, p. 70. See also Cummings interview for this encounter. The Cummings interview is reprinted in part in Moffett.

29 Hilton Kramer, "Fairfield Porter: An American Classic," *The New Criterion*, 1, 9; May 1983: pp. 1-7.

30 Cummings, p. 29.

31 Ibid., p. 31.

32 Ibid., pp. 14-15.

33 Ibid., p. 80.

34 Letter to Dick Freeman, October 26, 1973, courtesy of Ted Leigh.

35 Letter to Allen C. Dubois, April 8, 1963. Archives of American Art, Smithsonian Institution. Microfilm roll D-176, frame 444.

36 Cummings, p. 51.

37 "Class Content in American Abstract Painting," 1962; Downes, p. 253.

38 Downes, p. 170.

39 Ibid., p. 90.

40 Ibid., pp. 36-37.

41 Ibid., p. 90.

42 Letter to Edward B. Henning, in Henning, "South of his House, north of his House: *Nyack*, a Painting by Fairfield Porter." *Bulletin of The Cleveland Museum of Art,* 53, 3, March 1971: pp. 85-90.

43 Cummings, p. 14.

44 Ibid., p. 81.

45 Rackstraw Downes, interview with Emmie Donadio, in *Fairfield Porter and Rackstraw Downes: The Act of Seeing*. Christian A. Johnson Gallery, Middlebury College, 1991.

46. Finkelstein, op. cit.

47 Cummings, p. 89.

48 Ibid., p. 91.

49 In conversation with the author, July, 1991.

50 Downes, p. 259.

51 Ibid., p. 37.

CHRONOLOGY

Michele White

1907
Born in Winnetka, Illinois on June 10, the fourth of five children. His father was James Porter, an architect of private means. rness Porter, interested her children in art and writing. Both of the Porters were involved in politics. They raised their children as atheists.

1913
The Porter family spends their first summer at Great Spruce Head Island in Maine, which they have purchased as a summer retreat. His father designs and builds a house and other buildings which later appear regularly in Fairfield's paintings: "If I paint this house, I'm also painting a portrait of my father." As a child he experiments with open air sketching in pastels and watercolor while on the island. Porter is to spend nearly every summer of his life on Great Spruce Head.

1922
Travels to Europe with his family, where he sees paintings by Titian, Veronese, and Turner.

1923
After graduating from New Trier Township high school in Winnetka, spends a year at Milton Academy.

1924–1925
Travels to Norway and the British Isles. At the National Gallery, London he sees Leonardo's *Virgin of the Rocks*. Enters Harvard University, his father's alma mater. His brother is already in medical school at Harvard. Studies art history and fine arts with Arthur Pope and Arthur Kingsley Porter. Studies philosophy with Alfred North Whitehead. At Great Spruce Head this summer, Fairfield takes a few painting lessons.

1927
During the summer, travels to France with his brother Edward; they meet their brother Eliot in Paris. Porter travels on to Germany and Russia. In Moscow he sees the Shchukin Collection of Modern Art and the Morozov Collection. Porter meets Trotsky and is influenced by the work of Dostoyevsky, Chekov, and Tolstoy. While in Crimea he paints the Black Sea.

1928–1930
In 1928 Porter graduates from Harvard with a Bachelor of Science degree. He does not receive a Bachelor of Arts degree because he chooses not to take the required Latin courses. In the Harvard Class Album, he lists painting as his future profession. The time he spent in Russia stimulates an interest in socialism. Studies at The Art Students League in New York City, taking classes with Boardman Robinson and Thomas Hart Benton.

1931–1932
Travels to Europe with his mother. In the fall of 1931 Porter lives in Florence. He spends time in Italy copying paintings in the Uffizi Gallery and Palazzo Pitti. He sees Leonardo's Last Supper, the Giotto frescoes in the Arena Chapel, and Mantegna's frescoes in the Church of the Eremitani. He sees works by Piero della Francesca. Through John Walker, a friend from Harvard, Porter meets Bernard Berenson, whose aesthetic theories he had become aware of at Harvard. Under the influence of Berenson, Porter begins to look at Velásquez. He works on

illustrations for Dostoyevsky's *The Possessed*. He prints a lithograph from this series in Rome in 1932. Porter begins to study Russian. Visits collections in Dresden, Munich, Madrid, and Barcelona. He returns to New York via Paris and London. Upon his return he settles in New York City and marries the poet Anne Channing. They have five children: John born 1934; Laurence born 1936; Jeremy born 1941; Katherine born 1949; and Elizabeth born 1956.

1932
Honeymoon car tour of the South. The Porters visit friends in the Adirondacks. Porter has a car accident. Upon their return to New York they move to 122 Washington Place.

1933
Studies anatomy at Cornell University School of Medicine. Paints his first mural commission, for his in-laws.

1934
During the Depression he becomes involved with socialism and politics. The mural *Turn Imperialist War into Civil War* is commissioned by the Socialist party. Joins the Fresco Painters Guild. He teaches at Rebel Arts and is employed by them to decorate Madison Square Garden for an ILGWU event. Moves to 70 Bank Street. Has a painting accepted into an exhibition at The Pennsylvania Academy of the Fine Arts. Socializes with Paul Rosenfeld, who would later influence Porter's criticism.

1935
"Murals for Workers" is published in a socialist publication. It is Porter's first published art criticism. Porter lives in Croton-on-Hudson, New York, and in New York City. Works in studio near Union Square.

1936–1939
Meets Elaine and Willem de Kooning. He was to collect paintings by de Kooning. Porter works on illustrations for *Poems for a Dime* and *Poems for 2 Bits*, vanguard verse magazines created by John Brooks Wheelwright. Moves back to Winnetka where he lives in his grandmother's house until 1939.

1937
Shows a painting in the Annual Exhibition of Painting and Sculpture at The Art Institute of Chicago.

1938
Meets László Moholy-Nagy. Sees exhibition of Vuillard and Bonnard at The Art Institute of Chicago. He is influenced by Bonnard's paintings, especially the later works. He begins to emulate Vuillard, whose approach to painting seemed natural to him. Meets John Marin, whose work he greatly admires. Sees a show of Marin's work at Alfred Stieglitz's gallery, An American Place.

1939
Two paintings of Porter's are accepted into The Art Insitute of Chicago's *Forty-Second Annual Exhibition by Artists of Chicago and Vicinity*. Father dies. Moves to Peekskill, New York. Meets Clement Greenberg. De Kooning, who is painting the *Women*, is later told by Greenberg that he can't paint that way today.

1940
Visits John Marin in Maine.

1941
Meets Rudolph Burckhardt, who is to photograph many of Porter's paintings. Associates with the *Partisan Review* circle. Has another car accident.

1942–1943
Moves back to New York City. Receives an inheritance from his father. Buys a house on East 52nd Street, where he lives for seven years. Is employed as an industrial designer by the U.S. Navy. Quits after VJ Day.

1945–1946
Studies at Parsons School of Design with Jacques Maroger, who introduces him to the oil painting medium which he uses from then on, although in the sixties he will experiment briefly with acrylics. Meets Belgian painter Georges van Houten.

1948
Sees Bonnard retrospective at The Museum of Modern Art.

1949
Moves to Southampton, New York. In the Hamptons and New York City he associates with a large group of painters and poets. Throughout the fifties he enjoys friendships with the poets Frank O'Hara, James Schuyler, John Ashbery, and Kenneth Koch. Close painter colleagues include Alex Katz, Robert Dash, Jane Freilicher, Neil Welliver, Jane Wilson, and Paul Georges.

1950
Has two paintings in a show at The Artist's Gallery in New York City. On Great Spruce Head Island, begins to experiment with a casein paint.

1951
Through Elaine de Kooning, becomes an editorial associate for *Art News*. He stays until 1958 and continues to contribute articles until 1967.

1952
Exhibits for the first time at Tibor de Nagy Gallery, New York. Porter had reviewed one of the gallery's first shows.

1954–1955
Second and third exhibitions at Tibor de Nagy Gallery.

1958
His show at Tibor de Nagy is reviewed by his friend James Schuyler, who will periodically live with the Porters from 1961 onward.

1959
Becomes art critic for *The Nation*. Is awarded the Longview Foundation award for his article in *The Nation* on Willem de Kooning. Exhibits in the Whitney Museum of American Art Annual in alternate years until 1967. Writes a monograph on Thomas Eakins for George Braziller.

1960–1961
Continues to write for *The Nation*, also contributes to *Art in America* and *Evergreen Review*.

c. 1962
Begins an experimentation with acylics which will continue into the mid-sixties. Many Porter canvases which are described as oil on canvas are actually painted with acrylic.

1964
Visiting artist at Skowhegan School of Painting and Sculpture, Maine. While giving a talk at Yale, meets Rackstraw Downes, who in 1979 edits *Art in Its Own Terms,* a collection of Porter's writings.

1965
Porter is nearly killed in another car accident when a Long Island Railroad train hits his car.

1966
Retrospective at The Cleveland Museum of Art. Teaches painting and lectures at Southampton College of Long Island University, New York. Lectures at Yale and Skowhegan. Begins visits annually to The Maryland Institute, College of Art.

1967
Speaks at the Creative Arts Festival at Kent State University in Ohio. Travels to Rome, Orvieto, Florence, Venice, Paris, and London. The Porters get a dog for their youngest child, Lizzie. Bruno, the family dog, appears in many of Porter's later paintings.

1968
Exhibits in the United States pavilion at the Venice Biennale. Breaks his arm while walking Bruno. Paul Cummings interviews Porter for the Archives of American Art at his home on Long Island.

1969
Instructor in art at Queens College, New York.

1969–1970
Professor and artist in residence, Amherst College, Amherst, Massachusetts. Porter arranges a show of his own work at the college.

1970
When John Meyers and Tibor de Nagy dissolve their partnership, Porter moves to Knoedler rather than choosing between them. Gives the commencement address and receives an honorary degree from The Maryland Institute, College of Art. Shows his *Literary Portraits* at Gotham Book Mart. Begins to work on a series of lithographs.

1971
Moves to Hirschl & Adler when problems arise at Knoedler. One-person exhibition at The Parrish Art Museum, Southampton, New York.

1972
One-person exhibition at Hirschl & Adler Galleries, Inc., New York.

1973
Speaks at Joseph Cornell's memorial service. Designs book jacket for Kenneth Koch's *Rose, Where Did You Get That Red*. Porter had previously designed jackets for other friends' work.

1974
Visiting artist at Skowhegan School of Painting and Sculpture, Maine. One-person exhibition at Hirschl & Adler Galleries, Inc., New York. Retrospective at The Heckscher Museum, Huntington, New York, an exhibition of works from his entire career. Starts teaching at School for Visual Arts, New York.

1975
Works mainly in watercolors. On September 18, age 68, he dies in Southampton, New York.

1

Seated Boy. c. 1938

2

Cityscape. c. 1945

3

Wildflowers. c. 1948

4

Chair, c. 1949

5

Painting Materials. 1949

6
Studio Interior. 1951

27

F. Porter 52

7

Laurence Typing. 1952

8
Katie and Jacob in the Yard . 1953

10
Lunch under the Elm Tree. 1954

9
Lawn Scene. 1953

11

Armchair on Porch. 1955

12
Katie and Anne. 1955

13
Trail. c. 1955

14

Portrait of Elaine de Kooning. 1957

15

Still Life. 1958

16

Chrysanthemums. 1958

35

17

Anne, Lizzie, and Katie. 1958

18
A. K. J. 1959

19
East 11th Street. c. 1960

21
Calm Morning. 1961

38

20

Lizzie with Wild Roses. 1960

22
Rocking Horse. 1962

23
Primroses. c. 1963

27
Six O'Clock. 1964

24
Short Walk. 1963

25
The Screen Porch. 1964

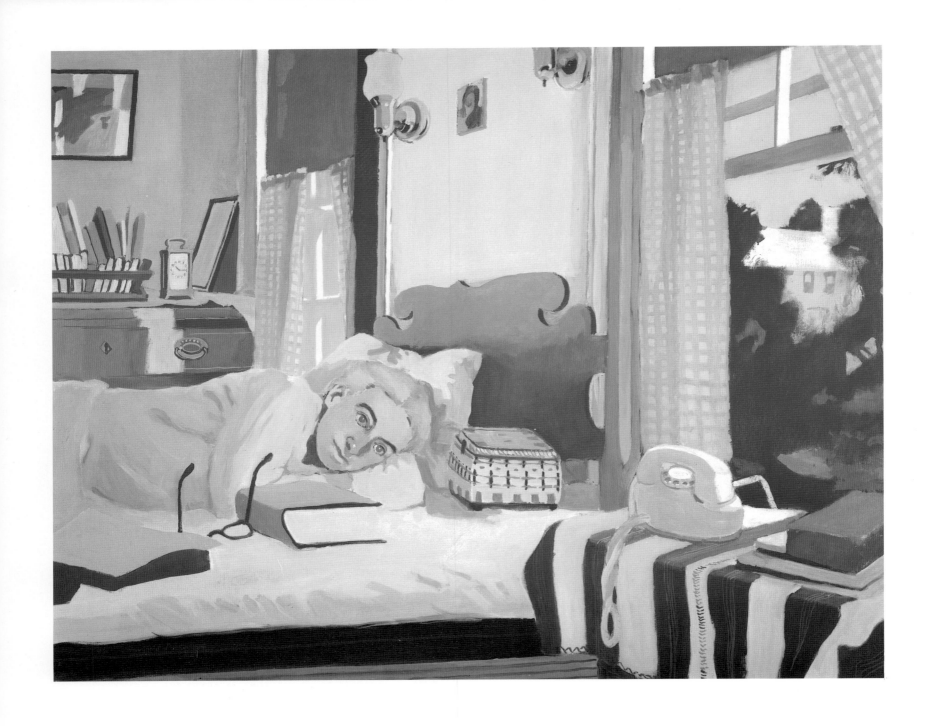

26
July Interior. 1964

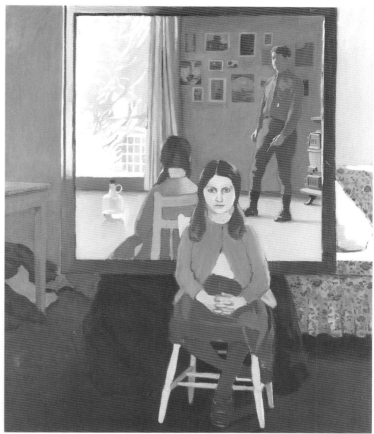

28
Still Life with Standing Figure. 1964

32
The Mirror. 1966

29

The Living Room. 1964

46

30
Morning Landscape. 1965

33
Early Morning. 1966

48

31
Anne. 1965

34

Penobscot Bay with Peak Island. 1966

35
Nyack. 1966-67

36
View towards the Studio. 1967

37

Anne in a Striped Dress. 1967

38
Jane and Elizabeth. 1967

39
The Wood Road. 1967-68

40
Self-Portrait in the Studio. 1968

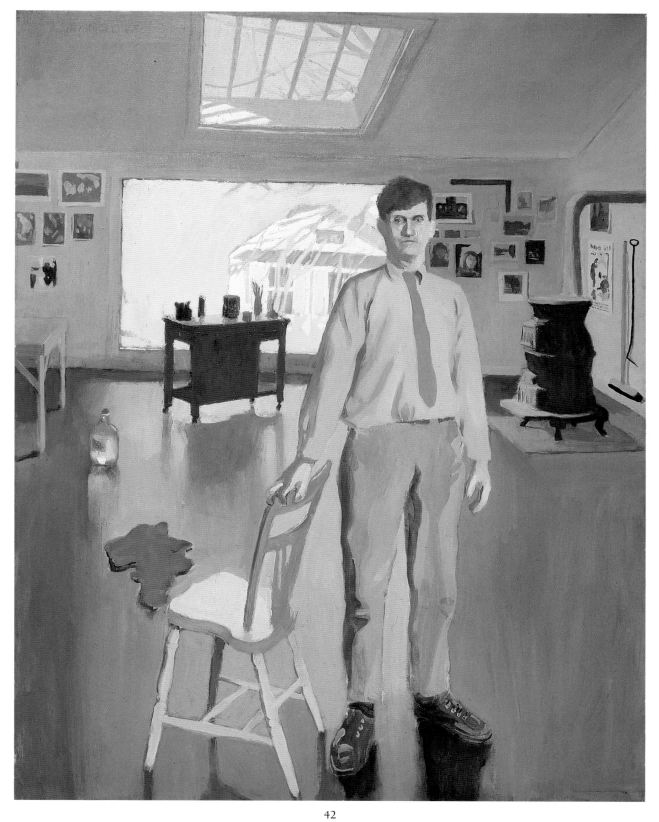

42

Self-Portrait. 1968

41
Columbus Day. 1968

58

44
Island Farmhouse. 1969

45

Amherst Campus No. 1. 1969

43

Boathouse and Lobster Pots. 1968-72

46

Clearing Weather. 1969

48
View of Barred Islands. 1970

47
South Meadow from the Beach. c. 1970

49
The Campus. 1970.

51
Aline by the Screen Door. 1971

50

Portrait of a Girl. 1971

52

Under the Elms. 1971

53

Snow—South Main Street. c. 1972

54
Late Afternoon—Snow. c. 1972

55

Self-Portrait. 1972

56

The Ocean. 1972

57

The Beginning of the Fields. 1973

58
Lizzie, Guitar and Christmas Tree, No. 1. 1973

63
Anne in Doorway. 1974

62
Blue Landscape. 1974

59

Sunrise on South Main Street. 1973

60

The Dock. 1974

61

The Harbor— Great Spruce Head. 1974

64
Yellow Sunrise. 1974

65
The Privet Hedge. 1975

A PAINTER OBSESSED BY BLUE

Fairfield Porter

No color isolates itself like blue.
If the lamp's blue shadow equals the yellow
Shadow of the sky, in what way is one
Different from the other? Was he on the verge of a discovery
When he fell into a tulip's bottomless red?
Who is the mysterious and difficult adversary?

If he were clever enough for the adversary
He should not have to substitute for blue,
For a blue flower radiates as only red
Does, and red is bottomless like blue. Who loves yellow
Will certainly make in his life some discovery
Say about the color of the sky, or another one.

That the last color is the difficult one
Proves the subtlety of the adversary.
Will he ever make the difficult discovery
Of how to gain the confidence of blue?
Blue is for children; so is the last yellow
Between the twigs at evening, with more poignancy than red.

A furnace with a roar consumes the red
Silk shade of a lamp whose light is not one
Like birds' wings or valentines or yellow,
Able to blot out the mysterious adversary
Resisted only by a certain blue
Illusively resisting all discovery.

Did it have the force of a discovery
To see across the ice a happy red
Grown strong in heart beside intensest blue?
In this case the blue was the right one,
As a valentine excludes the adversary,
That will return again disguised in yellow.

If it were possible to count on yellow
Dandelions would constitute discovery:
But all at once the sudden adversary
Like a nightmare swallows up the red,
To dissipate before the starry one,
The undefended wall of blue.

Blue walls crumple under trumpets of yellow
Flowers—one unrepeatable discovery—
And red prevails against the adversary.

From Fairfield Porter: The Collected Poems with Selected Drawings.
Edited by John Yau with David Kermani. New York: Tibor de Nagy Editions,
The Promise of Learning, Inc. (1985). Courtesy of Tibor de Nagy Gallery.

FAIRFIELD PORTER IN HIS OWN WORDS

Edited by Malama Maron-Bersin

All references are excerpts.

LETTER TO TOM
December 19, 1955

Anyway, what I like in painting and in writing is sensitiveness for the innate value of colors (concrete colors, the ones that are actually used in a painting) and for the innate value of words, of course the concrete ones that are used. In writing, there must be enough space, or perhaps I should say interval, between the nouns, adjectives and verbs; and in painting, enough space (or interval) between the colors, so that each one is in its appropriate place. Edwin Muir, in the introduction to his translation of *The Castle*, said that Kafka's style was one that used a small vocabulary, and its excellence depended on the exact placement of each word...

Drawing is too easy, or at least as it is considered: I think there is a comparable business about value in drawing in which the line serves to define and place accurately interior areas. Anne has a word for a kind of writing she admires, which is: transparency. This has nothing to do with making something clearly understandable as an idea. She said about the poems of John Ashbery that she admired that he lucidly shows you something that is a mystery. Transparency is the opposite of muddiness, and in a lot of painting that may be graphically interesting, there is a lot of muddiness; the colors though bright, are dispensable. This is a muddiness of perhaps a higher order than when the colors are not even bright. Sometimes colors are exchangeable; this is perhaps analogous to ambiguity in grammar, or, to force the comparison, perhaps the analogy is when a color occupies (apparently) more than one position, that is, forward or back, in relationship to another, as in Cézanne...

I think my admiration for Elizabeth Bishop's poems, aside from the fact that she has a descriptive visual mind, and aside from the fact that she has humor and is not sentimental, comes from an admiration of her relaxed line which allows each word enough space to be savored properly for what it is; and this comes from knowing when to change as well as when to repeat, how to keep such a distance that you pay attention and can go on, as you might go over the surface of a canvas, and not get stuck by boring repetitions or boring variations. Balance here means not balance like on opposite sides of a scale, but a sense of proportion, of how much, how long, and in this sense I could say that Rothko lacks the "balance" of Matisse. He lacks his sense of proportion: I have usually got the idea too soon; and he does not hold my interest. I could say this of Kline, too, very often. Rothko is not "unbalanced" because he is simple, but because the individual quality of value of his two colors are not sensitive enough.

Fairfield Porter Papers. Owned by Mrs. Fairfield Porter. Microfilmed by Archives of American Art, Smithsonian Institution (roll 2675, frames 141-142).

LETTER TO ALLEN C. DUBOIS
April 8, 1963

When I paint I try not to see the object as what it is; I try to see only very concrete shapes which have no association except as themselves. I try not to know what is there, but only to see where one thing (color, tone, value) ends and another begins, and also to see its, perhaps it would be accurate enough to say, texture. I don't mind anyone else seeing things and animals etc., if it doesn't annoy them. I suppose you see these shapes, because I, in my effort to see very specific shapes, though of what I don't care, do make these shapes insofar as I make them concrete, like recognizable other objects...

I have always had a feeling about shapes, not that they resembled other ones, but that they had character. I used to feel not at all unpleasantly that such inanimate objects had awareness of me—awareness without emotion, without criticism, that they *knew*. Maybe that is why I now see chairs not so much in the ordinary function of things that have a kind of life, which is not anthropomorphic nor in the form of animals, but a material life, quite indifferent to the animal or vegetable world, or as indifferent to these worlds as matter is to animals, people and plants, an indifferent thing.

Fairfield Porter Papers. Owned by David Soyer. Microfilmed by Archives of American Art, Smithsonian Institution (roll D-176, frame 444).

From the Second Annual "Festival of the Arts," Southampton College, Long Island University

CAN ART BE TAUGHT?
April 6, 1965

The abstract naturalist painter who wishes not to be realistic and at the same time communicate nature, produces something that unconsciously implies that the nature of nature is that it is chaotic; but the photograph reveals specific structure, that is, wholeness. I do not suggest that the artist should try to imitate photography. This won't get wholeness any more than an imitation of nature, for what is whole is unique and cannot be reproduced; and it cannot be found in pursuing a comparison with something outside itself, as nature, because this would necessarily make it partial... The opposition between realism and abstraction is a surface one. Where it is, there is a presence, like a person, an acknowledgment of a separate entity. A realistic painting refers to an outside presence of nature: a non-objective painting has its own presence...

The presence in a painting is like the presence a child feels and recognizes in things and the way they relate, like a doorknob, the slant of a roof or its flatness, or the personality of a tool. Art does not succeed by compelling you to like it, but by making you feel this presence in it. Is someone there? This someone can be impersonal. It is not a question of finding faces in the linoleum.

Fairfield Porter Papers. Owned by Mrs. Fairfield Porter. Microfilmed by Archives of American Art, Smithsonian Institution (roll 1311, frames 588, 591, 592).

When did you make that discovery?

After the last war, there was a show of paintings from the Kaiser Friedrich Museum at the Metropolitan and there were some Velázquez *infantas*. I'd seen them before in Berlin. I was beginning to be interested in what you can do with paint—what is the quality of paint, what is its nature. And I admired the liquid surface of Velázquez. And what might be called his understatement, though I don't like that word. The impersonality—I don't know what word to use. He leaves things alone. It isn't that he copies nature; he doesn't impose himself upon it. He is open to it rather than wanting to twist it. Let the paint dictate to you. There's more there than there is in willful manipulation. I used to like Dostoevsky very, very, very much. Now I prefer Tolstoy for the same reason. He is like Velázquez to me.

What I like in painting—partly what I like in painting—is to rationalize what I like. The artist doesn't know what he knows in general; he only knows what he knows specifically. And what he knows in general or what *can* be known in general becomes apparent later, through what he has had to put down. That to me is the most interesting art form. You are not quite in control of nature; you are a part of nature. It doesn't mean that you are helpless, either. It means that the whole question in art is to be wide awake, to be as attentive as possible, for the artist and for the person who looks at it or listens to it...

Do you think that reviewing had an effect on your painting?

Yes. It did have an effect on my painting. Not just writing, but looking at things. I would think about something that I was writing about, and then I would think: If this is the way, why are they doing such and such? Then I'd have a look at my own painting and think: Why am I doing this? Why can't I do it differently?...

How were the early paintings painted?

They were painted in that Benton manner. He said reality is a series of hollows and bumps. He had an elaborate technique that was completely worthless, I think. It had no sense, no sensuousness as far as the medium is concerned. After all, a painting is made of paint. Benton is one of those painters who seems to be trying to overcome that, as though that were an unfortunate drawback. I suppose I was thinking that what I had to do was to learn how to paint. And there wasn't anybody who could teach me. I just had to learn it. So I set about copying the way things looked, trying to get the concept of reality down. Franz Kline once told about a class he had. A lady said to him, "I don't know what to do with this painting." He said, "Well, where you see green put down green, and where you see blue put down blue." And that is true. And it's very hard to do. He hasn't really explained anything, or he's explained everything. One or the other. Nothing or everything...

Do you think that painting is more of an emotional expression than an intellectual one?

No, I don't think it's more emotional or more intellectual. I think it's a way of making the connection between yourself and everything. You connect yourself to everything that includes yourself by the process of painting. And the person who looks at it gets it vicariously. If you follow music you vicariously live the composer's efforts.

*Excerpted from the book **Artists In Their Own Words** by Paul Cummings. Copyright ©1979. Reprinted with permission from St. Martin's Press, Inc., New York, NY.*

Art shows that diversity is not chaos but the shape of the way things are; for there cannot be relationships without differences, quality without character, or transitions without distinctions. It says that reality is diverse, distinct and specific. This is what you live with.

Fairfield Porter Papers. Owned by Mrs. Fairfield Porter. Microfilmed by Archives of American Art, Smithsonian Institution (roll 2676, frame 10).

A good work of art can in its entirety be represented only by itself.
    —Tolstoy

Figure painting and especially portraiture contradicts twentieth-century aesthetic dogma. Alex Katz said that when you paint a portrait the difficulty is that you have to get a likeness *and* make the paint go across the canvas. This implies a paradoxical combination: that there is nothing of art in the first necessity, and nothing but art in the second. I intend to argue that there is no paradox, and to think that there is, is to misunderstand art...
A good portrait presents this irreducible reality that the artist's vision and sense of order are one. This quality was described by Francis Bacon referring to the Rembrandt self-portrait at Aix, in which the "mystery of fact is conveyed by an image being made out of non-rational marks," and by Giacometti, speaking of his own work: "I worked from the model throughout the day from 1935 to 1940. Nothing was like what I imagined it to be. A head (I soon left the figure aside, it was too much) became an object completely unknown and without dimensions." A portrait by Vuillard presents the fact of the relationship of facts and the unexpectedness of the most ordinary transitions between them. It adds up to a world whose quality, as Claude Roger-Marx more or less put it, is of one in which "The habitual lives in an enchanted domain." The reality discovered by Giacometti is that the minuteness of man marks a beginning for the immensity of space.

Fairfield Porter Papers. Owned by Mrs. Fairfield Porter. Microfilmed by Archives of American Art, Smithsonian Institution (roll 1311, frames 874, 880).

Whenever I talk to art students, in Amherst, Baltimore or Illinois all this year, I tell them that I think (to alter Thoreau) that in the artistic impulse is the preservation of the world. What I mean is that the artistic impulse is what makes one look at things for themselves, not as useful. It means to particularize instead of to generalize. It is generalization that has led to the harm that is done. And in this connection I am opposed to Bucky Fuller's ideas: he thinks always in general terms, for instance, he doesn't live anywhere, just on spaceship Earth. He wants to homogenize the earth, just like Robert Moses. And then people become distinguished from each other only to the same extent that one mass-produced screw is different from another, and details are only something to count, not to pay further attention to: quantity takes the place of character. He thinks of people only in the mass, only as replaceable parts of a machine.

From the Porter Family Archives, courtesy Mrs. Fairfield Porter.

STATEMENT FOR HIRSCHL & ADLER EXHIBITION CATALOGUE

Whenever I make a somewhat different painting, someone is likely to ask, "Is that a new direction?" They want to know what you are planning next. But I think this question arises from the misconception that what is interesting in painting are the ideas it expresses. Painters are concerned with things. The most prominent things in the painter's experience are right in front of him, like the paint on the canvas. It is better if he does not achieve a plan, and that the painting eludes him, with a life of its own. The painting unfolds, gradually and with difficulty, and he doesn't quite know what it is even for a while after he stops painting it. Then it falls into place for him, or it doesn't, but for another person who looks at it, it may have a peculiar character right away. So far as it has merit, a painting is a fact, arbitrary and individual.

*Excerpted from Fairfield Porter's personal statement for the catalogue **Recent Works by Fairfield Porter**, Hirschl & Adler Galleries, Inc., 1974. Reprinted by permission.*

ESSAY ON WILLEM DE KOONING

The phrase "abstract-expressionist" is now seen to mean "paintings of the school of de Kooning" who stands out from them as Giotto stood out from his contemporary realists who broke with the Byzantine conventions of Siena. The paintings are very big, approximately square; or if small, in the same big scale; in very broad strokes of a house painter's wide brushes, with a dry speed and some spatter; in deep ultramarine, a brownish pink, a very high-keyed yellow green, a cool bright yellow, white and a little black. They represent nothing, though landscape, not figures or still life, is suggested. The colors are intense—not "bright," not "primary"—but intensely them-selves, as if each color had been freed to be. The few large strokes, parallel to the frame and at V angles, also have this freed quality. So does the simple organization, the strange but simple color, the directions and identification with speed. And in the same way that the colors are intensely themselves, so is the apparent velocity always exactly believable and appropriate. There is that elementary principle of organization in any art that nothing gets in anything else's way, and everything is at its own limit of possibilities. What does this do to the person who looks at the paintings? This: the picture presented of released possibilities, of ordinary qualities existing at their fullest limits and acting harmoniously together—this picture is exalting. That is perhaps the general image. The paintings also remind one of nature, of autumn, say, but autumn essentially, released from the usual sentimental and adventitious load of personal and irrelevant associations.

*Excerpted from Fairfield Porter, "Willem de Kooning," **The Nation** magazine. © 1959 The Nation Company, Inc. Reprinted with permission.*

"ART AND KNOWLEDGE"

Sometimes people ask for standards by which to measure art, in order to be able to say that one thing is art, and another is not. The psychologist E.L. Thorndike contends, "whatever exists at all, exists in some amount," implying that art is measurable, or that it does not exist at all. Being used to explanation, we expect that when we ask what something is, the answer will place it in causality. Art has so much variety that it is tempting to try to find a common denominator. But the denominator is vitality, whose logic is inside itself. You can follow inner logic; you follow your vitality, you do not tow it behind you. Something is either alive or it is not. You can measure an amount of energy, but not aliveness, which, like a chemical reaction, has the quality of wholeness

The wholeness of life is neither the result of consciousness nor arrived at through decision. When New England was our western frontier the wholeness of life in Massachusetts centered on the individual who did almost everything for himself to live comfortably in the wilderness, like Robinson Crusoe on his island. His wished to exclude art from what he expressed, and being consciously anti-artistic, he could not see how artistic this life was, both in small things expressing it and in itself as a whole. In the same period, life at the French court, with no regard for comfort, attempted the magnificent burden of an earthly imitation of the hierarchy of heaven. And in order to express this consciously artistic and disciplined wholeness, French seventeenth-century art was as systematic as the law. But only the breakdown of this discipline and control resulted in its greatest artistic expression, namely tragedy.

As the wholeness of life eludes control, so the wholeness of art eludes the control of the artist. The realist thinks he knows ahead of time what reality is, and the abstract artist what art is, but it is in its formality that realist art excels, and the best abstract art communicates an overwhelming sense of reality.

Excerpted from "Art and Knowledge" by Fairfield Porter, ART NEWS, February, 1966, courtesy of the publisher.

"AGAINST IDEALISM"

The opposition between "realism" and "abstraction" is a misleading one. Both realists and abstractionists think they embody an ideal of art of which each work is the shadow: the realist making a reflection of the natural world and the abstractionist making a reflection of the world of ideas in the largest sense, which of course includes non-verbal ideas. Both think that what is real about art exists in the realm of Whitehead's "eternal objects" and no matter how much either one pretends to prefer either reality or unreality (like Clive Bell), this reality or unreality is an eternal object which an artist of whatever persuasion constantly refers to whenever he makes something. So is the opposition between "Humanism" and whatever a humanist thinks is non-humanist, unclear. It can mean, for an artist who wants to represent appearances, a preference for representing the human figure. It can also mean putting concern for man's welfare ahead of indifference to it. Such art chooses a content of social consciousness, and such a content in turn usually implies a criticism of the social order. This art wavers between a satire that is most effectively put into words, and sentimentality. Yet it is not possible for an artist to put into his products anything that remains untouched by the artist's nature.

Excerpted from "Against Idealism" by Fairfield Porter, **Art & Literature,** *Spring, 1966. Reprinted with permission.*

MIND, MATTER, MODERN ART AND METAPHYSICS

The mind which looks twice at the same trees sees nothing but the tree. The mind which looks twice at the same art, say even one of the first neanderthal deer of hunters, sees the art increased by intervening experience: perhaps just the intervening experience of one life but also possibly by the intervening experience of many generations.

Fairfield Porter Papers. Owned by Mrs. Fairfield Porter. Microfilmed by Archives of American Art, Smithsonian Institution (roll 1311, frame 869).

THE CLASS CONTENT OF MODERN PAINTING

The essential content of any painting is its vitality, and when it does not represent any object outside the painting, you see the state of the soul of the artist. Of course this is also visible in representational painting too, though the subject may distract you from it. The professional state of soul is manipulative. The professional thinks of an end, and skill is his means. The non-professional is lost in the process and his ends are not separate from his means. The non-professional acts like an artist for no reason at all; the professional uses art, and artistry may be his aim. The professional non-objective painter uses his talents partly to separate himself from others: the non-professional is contemplative. Contemplation is a mood of wonder and it is receptive.

Fairfield Porter Papers. Owned by Mrs. Fairfield Porter. Microfilmed by Archives of American Art, Smithsonian Institution (roll 1311, frame 629).

UNTITLED MANUSCRIPT

The artistic impulse is concerned with the arbitrary and the particular, and it does not put method ahead of experience. It does not choose between particulars and is undisturbed by the arbitrariness of facts. Logic though is also concerned with an arbitrariness but one that comes from method, that compels the user to suppress facts insusceptible to generalization, facts, as it were, that have not been checked by translation into a mediating form.

Fairfield Porter Papers. Owned by Mrs. Fairfield Porter. Microfilmed by Archives of American Art, Smithsonian Institution (roll 1311, frame 859).

WRITINGS ABOUT FAIRFIELD PORTER

Edited by Malama Maron-Bersin

There is something very hardheaded and unsentimental about Porter's work, an honest appraisal of what the eye sees. Nature is analyzed and offered as patches of paint which fit together. There are no tricks, no obvious patterns, no composing by the line, yet everything holds together.

The children are never alone because the furniture lives, too. Sometimes his acute appraisal seems to extend to the thoughts of the subjects. *Katy*, though a little girl having breakfast, is thinking about being a fish or a bird. The stove in *The Big Studio* is not displeased at being cast in the role of prima-donna.

Excerpted from "Reviews and Previews" by Lawrence Campbell, ART NEWS, October, 1952, courtesy of the publisher.

Composition, for Porter, is a conscious procedure, an advance of decisions which become more and more irrevocable as the work goes on: the subject (its size and position), the area around it to be included, color and its differentiation, linear continuity and similarity, distinctions of mass, these things are arrived at gradually through detailed decisions. But no part of the picture is finished before another: 'it should always have a look of beginning, of freshness'; and if a decision gives an area too much resolution, it is removed or altered...

In preparing for the final painting, he increased the detail of his perception rather than his perception of details, accomplishing this largely through distinctions of mass. He relies neither on spontaneity nor on originality of viewpoint. He does not paint a version of reality: there is something there which he can get "right" in art, with perseverance, insight and luck. "Art is the perception of differences rather than likenesses," but it is also involved in preserving the appearance of things so that these distinctions do not occur in a vacuum...

Fairfield Porter's paintings stand or fall by their composition: it is the literal meaning of his perceptions and he will do any number of versions of a motif to perfect its utterance. Perhaps it is only his insistence on presenting differences within the compositional perception which keeps his paintings from becoming abstractions and therefore facts, in the sense that a Mondrian is a fact. He is interested in the areas of forms, rather than their contours, and it is in the interior quality of areas that the distinctions between forms become most clear.

Excerpted from "Porter Paints a Picture" by Frank O'Hara, ART NEWS, January, 1955, courtesy of the publisher.

Although Porter works best when he paints what he sees, he also consciously reduces appearance to simplicities. Franz Kline once said that for him composition is the motion of the brush determining it, and Porter would agree with this, as also with what Whistler said about a painting being 'finished' from the very beginning.

Excerpted from "Reviews and Previews" by Lawrence Campbell, ART NEWS, November, 1960, courtesy of the publisher.

Porter now paints so well that his limitations don't seem to matter. They are an integral part of his art, and correcting them at this late date may upset the entire ecology of a style based on a system of checks and balances. If, for instance, his forms seem cramped, they are drawn out by a surprisingly, and even increasingly, sensuous painting style. If his color is a bit bleached, it is saved by the taciturn naturalness of feeling which, pervading each painting, rescues it from its picturesque inclinations. His sophisticated sense of form controls his drift to provincialism, which is also outflanked by a sense of subject that Hemingway might have called 'true.' I think it is a measure of Porter's quality that only an American could have painted this way, despite his obvious dependency on an older Europe via a more contemporary New York. To do what Porter has done, to overcome first the emotional prescriptions evident in a relatively static vision (though the paint moves) and then to overcome the pictorial obstacles this necessary modesty would impose, you have to be good. And Porter is good, one of the best. Not being the sensational or dramatic sort, he has had to wait until he was in his fifties and for a shift in public taste before his art caught on, as it seems to with this exhibition from which thirteen paintings had been sold at this writing.

Excerpted from "In the Galleries" by Sidney Tillim, Arts Magazine, February, 1962, courtesy of the publisher.

A propos of composition, he once said, 'The right use of color can make *any* composition work,' and that in fact the color is the composition. He likes a coherent, unmuddy, close adjustment of values, such as he found in Fra Angelico and in de Kooning: an adjustment in which the colors affect one another within the picture, and give it the fullness of range (the light within the room, the light outside the window) which the eye so much more readily grasps than does a camera. He paints air as light that shatters on surfaces in a spectrum that is, unlike a rainbow, consistent only to itself. One may know that the trunk of a sycamore scales off and discloses a creamy underbark, and that its shadow is stretched on grassblades whose myriads only a computer could tabulate, but the paint sees trunk and shadow as a continuity, a brown-violet beam which has no existence out of its context, but which is the thing truly seen.

Excerpted from "Immediacy is the Message" by James Schuyler, ART NEWS, March, 1967, courtesy of the publisher.

We are in the realm, then, of French art with a Yankee accent, of something called classical and Catholic and Mediterranean transmuted into something romantic and Protestant and Anglo-Saxon. Esthetically, the air is thinner here than in the art of the French masters, but this is true also of Hopper and Dickinson. The hedonism which is an abiding characteristic of the French painters Mr. Porter derives from come less easily to a Yankee sensibility. There is, in Mr. Porter's painting, an odd lack of sensuality— odd, because the style seems to derive from an interesting interplay of sensuality and analysis, and yet one of the terms of this exchange is so manifestly weaker than the other.

The element of analysis in Mr. Porter's painting is very strong, however; the formal construction of his pictures is always a superb feat of esthetic intelligence in itself. He is also very deft in representing a certain atmosphere, particularly a domestic atmosphere. But these strengths sometimes underscore a weakness, for his figures are somehow never equal in pictorial substance to the stuctures they occupy or to the atmosphere they are ostensibly designed to evoke. Except in those pictures—rarely his best—which are explicitly intended as portraits, the figures in Mr. Porter's pictures never seem quite necessary; the weight of expression is so obviously invested elsewhere—in the rendering of light, in the subtleties of texture and structure. Perhaps this is another aspect of his Yankee sensibility.

Excerpted from "An Art of Conservation," Hilton Kramer's review of a show of Fairfield Porter's art, Feb. 9, 1969. Copyright © 1969 by The New York Times Company. Reprinted by permission.

One does not think of Porter as being an especially audacious painter, and, technically speaking, he is not. More than anything else, he is an original and audacious thinker about art, and the quality of his thought is reflected in the perfectly natural, non-eccentric strangeness of his style. Specifically, he has been able, without compromising either his temperament or his ambition, to fashion a way of painting that communicates easily between the past and the present both of art and his own personal experience. He has been aided in this by a mind that, while generous to every expression of talent in others, maintains an instinctively stubborn resistance to our age's habit of assigning value on the basis of generalized criteria. It is no accident that in his work he has uncovered a live tradition that springs from artists commonly regarded as peripheral cases...

It takes intelligence to make art simply. It takes more intelligence than that to subsume the traces of one's intelligence in the art one makes—to avoid, that is, the merely intellectual. And this, it seems to me, is the special achievement of Fairfield Porter, a significant one in these times. Scarcely 'conservative'—because embarked on a continuing adventure of perception—his paintings celebrate the survival, in art, of personal feelings and, in society, of the happy, private life. The triumph of his austerely sensuous, determinedly spontaneous style, in an art world where little that has roots going deeper than a decade or so into the past seems to flourish, helps give an amplitude to one's experience of art in the present and a touch of wisdom to one's expectations of art's future. He is a marvellous painter, and he is indispensable.

Excerpted from "Recent Work by Fairfield Porter" by Peter Schjeldahl, in Fairfield Porter: An American Painter, Hirschl & Adler Galleries, Inc., New York, April 11–29, 1972. Reprinted by permission.

Subject matter must be normal in the sense that it does not appear sought after so much as simply happening to one. Porter's subjects are mostly immediate surroundings, his home either on South Main Street in Southampton or on Great Spruce Head Island in Maine, and their immediate environs, members of his family and close friends, and, occasionally, views of rather ordinary streets in New York. The presentation must not be heavy in the sense of an elaborate compositional apparatus, or in any heightening of an explicit attitude—dramatic, emotional, romantic, lyric—but rather straightforward and documentary. The typical, the idealized, and the logical are rejected in favor of the specific, informal, and unexpected. Technique also must be unstrained, bordering on the clumsy, without elegancies of drawing or matiére. Although Porter's work is to be described as painterly it is never sumptuous, where sumptuousness is an end in itself. His drawings are straightforward, spare, a little jocular in their immediacy and unpretentiousness. His watercolors are direct, tentative, frequently incomplete, and never exhibiting a flashy use of the medium...

In the same way that Vuillard's Nabi decorative work provided him with a compulsion and a standard of formal integration, so for Porter Vuillardism formed the underpinning of a cultivated and concentrated awareness of structure which he turned increasingly to his own uses. The basis of this structure is color, which in his hands functioned in a very special way. His color is never imitative in the sense of literal correspondence, but rather, and most especially in those cases where it seems most documentary, rigorously synthetic. Color always makes a specific, autonomous statement, derived only partially from an analysis of the sight seen, and more largely due to a combination of reduction and distortion to a precise and quite small set of carefully quantified and qualified components. By 'qualified' is meant both specific, rather unusual kinds of colors and a discerning sense of the way their appearance is modified by their mutual interaction.

*Excerpted from "The Naturalness of Fairfield Porter" by Louis Finkelstein, **Arts Magazine**, May, 1976, courtesy of the publisher.*

The post-Impressionists, and especially Cézanne, seemed to him to have imposed themselves too much on the individuality and structure of nature, and he felt their art represented a falling off from the Impressionists and Vuillard. In fact, Porter usually saw the whole period from Cézanne to World War II in negative terms. He felt it had been too 'conceptual,' too involved with ideas. According to Porter, it is only with Abstract Expressionism that we again have a kind of painting like Impressionism that is both empirical and respectful of its means. This was Porter's reading of modern art. He felt that it was Vuillard, not Cézanne, who had 'made of Impressionism something solid and durable like the art of the museums.' 'Vuillard organized Impressionist discoveries about color and pigments into a coherent whole.' Or Vuillard was more 'coherent and orderly' than Monet. Now it can be said that more than Cézanne or Bonnard or Monet, Vuillard, especially the later Vuillard, kept to traditional perspective and drawing. He was innovative, fresh, personal, mostly in his handling of paint and in his unusual sense of color. Something like this could be said about Porter, too; he experienced what we think of as Vuillard's conservatism, a respect for the wholeness, uniqueness, and presence of the world.

*Excerpted from "The Art of Fairfield Porter" by Kenworth Moffett, in **Fairfield Porter/ Realist in an Age of Abstraction**, catalogue from an exhibition at the Museum of Fine Arts, Boston, 1983. Reprinted by permission.*

And I realized after such a long acquaintanceship that his paintings, which most people like but have difficulty talking about (Are they modern enough? Too French? Too pleasant? Hasn't this been done before?), are part of the intellectual fabric that underlay his opinions, his conversation, his poetry, his way of being. They are intellectual in the classic American tradition of the writers mentioned above because they have no ideas in them, that is, no ideas that can be separated from the rest. They *are* idea, or consciousness, or light, or whatever. Ideas surround them, but do not and cannot extrude themselves into the being of the art, just as the wilderness surrounds Stevens's jar in Tennessee: an artifact, yet paradoxically more natural than the 'slovenly' wilderness that approaches it, and from which it takes 'dominion.'...

In the same letter Porter quoted from memory a line of Wittgenstein that he felt central to his own view of aesthetics: 'Every sentence is in order as it is.' And he went on astonishingly to elaborate: 'Order seems to come from searching for disorder, and awkwardness from searching for harmony or likeness, or the following of a system. The truest order is what you already find there, or that will be given if you don't try for it. When you arrange, you fail.' I think it is in the light of statements like these that we must now look at Porter's painting, prepared to find the order that is already there, not the one that should be but the one that is.

Excerpted from "Respect for Things as They Are" by John Ashbery, in **Fairfield Porter/ A Realist Painter in an Age of Abstraction.** *Reprinted by permission.*

What does Porter's naturalness or informality consist of and how are these qualities compatible with intensity? His subjects are all drawn from the most normal experiences of daily life, those that take place in or around the house or a short walk from it. They are moments of leisure. No work is shown, hardly even domestic chores, except for the work of the artist—Porter in his studio. Here he is not stretching a canvas or scrutinizing his own face; he is in the act of looking, of beholding all parts of the field of vision equally and simultaneously. And it is this act of beholding that will become the issue. Where there are several people included in a picture, it is not for the sake of drama or psychological overtones; where there are objects, they have not

been arranged in order to be painted: They happened to be there. A view of the outdoors—one hesitates to use the word "landscape," it seems too formal, something already detached from the continuum of the everyday—does not celebrate some extraordinary spot, nor is there any feeling that it portrays a special moment like the one recorded in a haiku. A bush in blossom in Porter will bloom again tomorrow, or another one will. But though nothing is exceptional, everything is unique. Porter's pictures have what Boris Pasternak (a poet he admired) had in mind when he spoke of 'The endless repetition/Of unrepeatable days.'

Excerpted from "Fairfield Porter's Unrepeatable Days" by Rackstraw Downes, ART NEWS, April 1983. Courtesy of the author.

Fairfield undoubtedly is terribly interested in the paint. He is certainly not interested in the subject. The subject is only a pretext, only a background for the execution of the painting. I mean there is no subject in Fairfield's painting until he starts working on it. [When he paints a portrait] it is not a portrait in the conventional sense. And I think that it is very important and not all that well understood about Fairfield. He himself made a wonderful statement about it. He said that the artist who searches for subject matter is like someone who cannot get out of bed in the morning without understanding the meaning of life.

Excerpted from a statement by Rackstraw Downes in **Fairfield Porter and Rackstraw Downes: The Act of Seeing,** *brochure from an exhibition at The Christian A. Johnson Memorial Library, Middlebury College, Middlebury, Vermont, May 31–July 7, 1991. Reprinted by permission.*

LIST OF EXHIBITIONS
Peter Blank

Exhibition titles and dates have been included when they were confirmed by announcements, catalogues, or reviews.

Solo and Dual Exhibitions

1933 Theodore A. Kohn & Son, New York. May 1933. [Porter and Simeon Braguin].

1939 North Shore Art Center, Winnetka, Illinois.

1952 Tibor de Nagy, New York. Oct. 7-26.

1954 Tibor de Nagy. Apr. 13-May 1.

1955 Tibor de Nagy.

1956 Tibor de Nagy. Mar. 24-Apr. 21.

1958 Tibor de Nagy. Apr. 29-May 29.

1959 Rhode Island School of Design, Providence. Tibor de Nag
. Mar. 17-Apr. 4.

1960 Tibor de Nagy. Nov. 1-26

1961 Tibor de Nagy.

1962 Tibor de Nagy.

1963 University of Alabama, Tuscaloosa. University of Illinois, Champaign. Tibor de Nagy. Jan. 29-Feb. 16.

1964 Tibor de Nagy. Mar. 17-Apr. 11. John Russell Mitchell Gallery, Southern Illinois University, Carbondale, Illinois. "Fairfield Porter, Paintings." Nov. 1-27.

1965 Reed College, Portland, Oregon. Tibor de Nagy. "Fairfield Porter: Paintings." Feb. 16-Mar. 25.

1966 Tibor de Nagy. "Fairfield Porter: Recent Paintings." Feb. 15-March 5. The Cleveland Museum of Art. "Genre Art of Fairfield Porter." Aug. 9-Sept. 11.

1967 Kent State College, Kent, Ohio. Swarthmore College, Swarthmore, Pennsylvania. Trinity College, Hartford, Connecticut. Tibor de Nagy. "Fairfield Porter: Recent Paintings." Feb. 18-Mar. 16. Shepard Gallery, New York. "Fairfield Porter: Drawings: Studies for Paintings and Watercolors." Nov. 29-Dec. 16.

1968 Richard Gray Gallery, Chicago. "Fairfield Porter: New Paintings." Mar. 6-Apr. 6.

1969 Gross-McCleaf Gallery, Philadelphia. Tibor de Nagy. "Fairfield Porter: Recent Paintings." Jan. 25-Feb. 13. Colby College Art Museum. "Fairfield Porter: Paintings; Eliot Porter: Photographs." May 6-June 24.

1970 Tibor de Nagy. "Fairfield Porter." Apr. 4-23. Gotham Book Mart Gallery, New York. "Literary Portraits by Fairfield Porter." Dec. 14, 1970-Jan. 30, 1971.

1971 The Parrish Art Museum, Southampton, New York. "Fairfield Porter: Recent Paintings." July 2-28.

1972 Hirschl & Adler Galleries, New York. "Recent Work by Fairfield Porter." Apr. 11-29. Mount Royal Station Gallery, The Maryland Institute, College of Art, Baltimore. "An Exhibition of Paintings by Fairfield Porter." Oct. 20-Nov. 18.

1973 Harbor Gallery, Cold Spring Harbor, New York. "Fairfield Porter." Aug. 19-Sept. 15.

1974 Hirschl & Adler. "Recent Work by Fairfield Porter." Mar. 2-23. The Heckscher Museum, Huntington, New York. "Fairfield Porter: Retrospective Exhibition." Dec. 15, 1974-Jan. 26, 1975. Traveled to Queens Museum of Art, Flushing, New York; and The Montclair Art Museum, New Jersey.

1975 Jorgensen Auditorium Gallery, University of Connecticut, Storrs. "Fairfield Porter Paintings: 1955-1975." Sept. 29-Oct. 18. Brooke Alexander Gallery, New York. "Fairfield Porter: Watercolors 1973-1975." Dec. 2, 1975-Jan. 6, 1976.

1976 Hirschl & Adler. "Fairfield Porter: His Last Works: 1974-1975." May 4-28.

1977 Alpha Gallery, Boston. "Paintings by Fairfield Porter." Feb. 5-Mar. 2. Harbor Gallery, Cold Spring Harbor, New York. "Fairfield Porter (1907-1976)." Mar. 13-Apr. 16. The Parrish Art Museum, Southampton, New York. "Fairfield Porter's Maine." July 2-Sept. 11. Traveled to Colby College Art Museum, Waterville, Maine. Tibor de Nagy. "Fairfield Porter and Andrew Hudson [drawings]." Sept. 17-Oct. 6.

1978 Gross-McCleaf Gallery, Philadelphia. Suzanne Hilberry Gallery, Birmingham, Michigan. "Fairfield Porter." Mar. 25-Apr. 22. Esther Robles Gallery, Los Angeles. "Fairfield Porter: His Last Works 1974-1975." Oct. 3-27.

1979 Gross-McCleaf Gallery. Artist's Choice Museum, New York. Hull Gallery, Washington, D.C. "Fairfield Porter." Barridoff Galleries, Portland, Maine. "Fairfield Porter." July 23-Sept. 3. Hirschl & Adler. "Fairfield Porter: Figurative Painting." Nov. 3-Dec. 1. Mickelson Gallery, Washington, D.C. "Fairfield Porter 1907-1975: Prints and Paintings." Dec. 3, 1979-Jan. 28, 1980.

1980 Susanne Hilberry Gallery, Birmingham, Michigan. "Fairfield Porter: Paintings and Watercolors." Feb. 9-Mar. 8.

1981 Mead Art Museum, Amherst College, Amherst, Massachusetts. "Memories of Fairfield Porter." Apr. 7-May 7.

1982 The Parrish Art Museum, Southampton, New York. "Prints by Fairfield Porter." Apr. 18-June 6.

1983 Museum of Fine Arts, Boston. "Fairfield Porter: Realist Painter in the Age of Abstraction." Jan. 12-Mar. 13. Traveled to Greenville County Museum of

Art, South Carolina; The Cleveland Museum of Art; Museum of Art, Carnegie Institute, Pittsburgh; Whitney Museum of American Art, New York.

1984 Tibor de Nagy. "Fairfield Porter: Paintings & Drawings." May 26–June 20. Whitney Museum of American Art, Fairfield County, Stamford, Connecticut. "Fairfield Porter: Portraits." June 1–Aug. 22. Arts Club of Chicago. "Fairfield Porter: Paintings and Works on Paper." Nov. 12–Dec. 31.

1985 Hirschl & Adler Modern, New York. "Fairfield Porter, 1907–1975." Sept. 5–28.

1986 Katonah Gallery, Katonah, New York. "Fairfield Porter: The Late Watercolors." June 15–Aug. 10. Traveled to The Arkansas Arts Center, Little Rock; The Aspen Art Museum, Colorado.

1987 Marian Locks Gallery, Philadelphia. "Fairfield Porter: A Selection of Paintings, 1948–1974." The Parrish Art Museum, Southampton, New York. "Fairfield Porter: Paintings & Prints." Apr. 5–May 3.

1988 CompassRose Modern & Contemporary Art, Chicago. "Fairfield Porter: Pictures and Words: Inaugural Exhibition."

1991 The Christian A. Johnson Memorial Gallery, Middlebury College, Middlebury, Vermont. "Fairfield Porter and Rackstraw Downes: The Act of Seeing." May 31–July 7.

1992 Bertha and Karl Leubsdorf Art Gallery, Hunter College, New York. "Porter Pairings." Mar. 31–May 22.

1993 The Parrish Art Museum, Southampton, New York. "Fairfield Porter: An American Painter." June 26–Aug. 19. Traveled to Mead Art Museum, Amherst College, Massachusetts; Snite Museum of Art, University of Notre Dame, Notre Dame, Indiana; Albright–Knox Art Gallery, Buffalo, New York; Colby College Museum of Art, Waterville, Maine; Museum of Art, Fort Lauderdale, Florida.

Group Exhibitions

1934 Pennsylvania Academy of the Fine Arts, Philadelphia.

1937 The Art Institute of Chicago. "Annual Exhibition of Painting and Sculpture."

1939 Pennsylvania Academy of the Fine Arts, Philadelphia. Artists' Union, Chicago. The Art Institute of Chicago. "Forty-second Annual Exhibition by Artists of Chicago and Vicinity."

1950 Artist's Gallery, New York. January.

1951 New York (60 E. 9th St.). "9th Street Show."

1959 Whitney Museum of American Art, New York. "Annual Exhibition of Contemporary American Painting." Dec. 9, 1959–Jan. 31, 1960.

1961 Museum of Modern Art, New York. Yale University Art Gallery, New Haven. Dayton Art Institute, Ohio. Whitney Museum of American Art, New York. "Annual Exhibition 1961: Contemporary American Painting." Dec. 13, 1961–Feb. 4, 1962.

1962 University of Nebraska, Lincoln. Kansas City Art Institute, Missouri. Pennsylvania Academy of the Fine Arts, Philadelphia. National Institute of Arts and Letters, Washington, D.C. Hirschl & Adler Galleries. "Continuing Tradition of Realism."

1963 Colby College Art Museum, Waterville, Maine. "Maine and Its Artists." Whitney Museum of American Art, New York. "Annual Exhibition 1963: Contemporary American Painting." Dec. 11, 1963–Feb. 2, 1964.

1964 The Maryland Institute, College of Art, Baltimore. New York World's Fair, Flushing, New York.

1965 Old Hundred Museum, Ridgefield, Connecticut. University Art Museum, The University of New Mexico, Albuquerque. Gallery of Modern Art, New York. Whitney Museum of American Art, New York. "1965 Annual Exhibition of Contemporary Painting." Dec. 8, 1965–Jan. 30, 1966.

1966 Purdue University, West Lafayette, Indiana. Brooks Memorial, Memphis, Tennessee. Cincinnati Art Museum, Ohio.

1967 The Arkansas Arts Center, Little Rock. Akron Art Institute, Ohio. Wilmington Society of Fine Arts, Delaware. Flint Institute of Arts, Michigan. Whitney Museum of American Art, New York. "1967 Annual Exhibition of American Painting." Dec. 13, 1967–Feb. 4, 1968.

1968 Venice Biennale (34th), United States Pavilion, Venice, Italy. "The Figurative Tradition in Recent American Art." June 22–Oct. 20. Traveled to National Collection of Fine Arts, Washington, D.C.; Sheldon Memorial Art Gallery, Lincoln, Nebraska.

1970 Smith College Museum of Art, Northampton, Massachusetts. "Painterly Realism." Feb. 7–Mar. 1. The Heckscher Museum, Huntington, New York. " Artists of Suffolk County: part III: The Figurative Tradition." Sept. 25–Nov. 1. The Heckscher Museum, Huntington, New York. " Artists of Suffolk County: part IV: The New Landscape." Nov. 13–Dec. 7.

1972 M. Knoedler & Co., New York. "Lithographs by de Kooning, Fairfield Porter, Paul Waldman." The Heckscher Museum, Huntington, New York. "The Artists of Suffolk County: part VI: Contemporary Prints." July 16–Sept. 3.

1973 Randolph Macon Woman's College, Lynchburg, Virginia. Dayton Art Institute, Ohio. Harcus-Krakow Gallery, Boston. Joselyn Art Museum, Omaha; Sheldon Memorial Art Gallery, University of Nebraska, Lincoln. A Sense of Place: The Artist and the American Land." Sept. 23–Oct. 28. Exhibitions ran concurrently, each having unique entries. Both included one painting by Fairfield Porter.

1974 Kalamazoo Institute of Arts, Michigan. Country Art Gallery, Locust Valley, New York. The Cleveland Museum of Art, Ohio. "Aspects of the Figure." July 10–Sept. 1. Associated American Artists, New York. "New York, New York." Aug. 5–Sept. 30. Brooke Alexander Gallery. "New Editions by ... Fairfield Porter, ..." Sept. 14–Oct. 12.

1975 Carlton Gallery, New York. Ingber Gallery, New York. De Cordova Museum and Sculpture Garden, Lincoln, Massachusetts. "Candid Painting: American Genre 1950–1975." Oct. 12–Dec. 7.

1976 Artist's Choice Museum, New York. The Corcoran Gallery of Art, Washington, D.C. "America 1976: A Bicentennial Exhibition Sponsored by the United States Department of the Interior." Apr. 27–June 6. Traveled to Fogg Art Museum, Cambridge, Massachusetts; Minneapolis Institute of Arts, Minnesota; Milwaukee Art Center, Wisconsin; Fort Worth Art Museum, Texas; San Francisco Museum of Modern Art; High Museum of Art, Atlanta, Georgia; The Brooklyn Museum, New York. The Heckscher Art Museum, Huntington, New York. "Artists of Suffolk County: Part X: Recorders of History." May 9–June 20. Tibor de Nagy. "25th Anniversary Show: Part II." Dec. 4–31. Suzanne Hilberry Gallery, Birmingham, Michigan. "Opening Group Exhibition." Dec. 9, 1976–Jan. 15, 1977.

1977 Whitney Museum of American Art, New York. "Selections from the Lawrence Bloedel Bequest and Related Works from the Permanent Collection." Apr. 5–June 19. Whitney Museum of American Art, New York. "New York on Paper." Apr. 7–May 22. National Collection of Fine Arts, Washington, D.C. "25th National Exhibition of Prints." May 27–Sept. 18.

1978 Hirschl & Adler Galleries. "Selections 78." Worcester Art Museum, Massachusetts. "Two Decades of American Printmaking 1957–1977." Mar. 15–May 14. Neuberger Museum, State University of New York at Purchase. "In Celebration: Selections from the Private Collection of Roy R. and Marie S. Neuberger." Sept. 24–Nov. 26. Boston University Art Gallery. "Brooke Alexander: A Decade of Print Publishing." Nov. 27–Dec. 22.

1979 The Metropolitan Museum of Art, New York. "New Acquisitions in 20th–Century Art." Oct. 16, 1979–Jan. 30, 1980. Harbor Gallery, Cold Spring Harbor, New York. "A Selection of Great Prints: Vol. 4." Dec. 9, 1979–Feb. 28, 1980.

1980 Lubin House Gallery, Syracuse University, New York. "Tibor de Nagy: Works for the Personal Collection." Feb. 6–Mar. 21 1980. The Parrish Art Museum, Southampton, New York. "The Porter Family." May 18–July 13. Whitney Museum of American Art, New York. "The Figurative Tradition and the Whitney Museum of American Art: Paintings and Sculpture from the Permanent Collection." June 25–Sept. 28. The Philbrook Museum of Art, Tulsa, Oklahoma. "Realism, Photorealism." Oct. 5–Nov. 23. The Chrysler Museum, Norfolk, Virginia. "American Figure Painting: 1950–1980." Oct. 17–Nov. 30.

1981 Rutgers University Art Gallery, New Brunswick, New Jersey. "Realism and Realities: The Other Side of American Painting 1940–1960." Jan. 17–Mar. 26. Traveled to Montgomery Museum of Fine Arts, Alabama; Art Gallery, University of Maryland, College Park, Maryland. San Antonio Museum of Art. "Real, Really Real, Super Real: Directions in Contemporary American Realism." Mar. 1–Apr. 26. Traveled to Indianapolis Museum of Art, Indiana; Tucson Museum of Art, Arizona; Museum of Art, Carnegie Institute, Pittsburgh. Hirschl & Adler Contemporaries, New York. "The Contemporary American Landscape." May 2–29. Pennsylvania Academy of the Fine Arts, Philadelphia. "Contemporary American Realism Since 1960." Sept. 16–Dec. 13. Traveled to Virginia Museum of Fine Arts, Richmond; The Oakland Museum, California; Portugal; Germany.

1984 Guild Hall Museum, East Hampton, New York. "Art and Friendship: A Tribute to Fairfield Porter." Apr. 14–June 3. Traveled to Artists'Choice Museum, New York; New Britain Museum of American Art, Connecticut. The Parrish Art Museum, Southampton, New York. "Fairfield Porter & His Influences: Painting Naturally." Apr. 15–June 3.

1985 San Francisco Museum of Modern Art. "American Realism: Twentieth-Century Drawings and Watercolors from the Glenn C. Janss Collection." Nov. 7, 1985–Jan. 12, 1986. Traveled to De Cordova and Dana Museum, Lincoln, Massachusetts; Archer M. Huntington Art Gallery, University of Texas, Austin; Mary & Leigh Block Gallery, Northwestern University, Evanston, Illinois; Williams College Museum of Art, Williamstown, Massachusetts; Akron Art Museum, Ohio; Madison Art Center, Wisconsin.

1987 Rahr West Art Museum, Manitowoc, Wisconsin. "Still Life: Painting Sculpture Drawing." July 26–Sept. 6.

1988 Newport Harbor Art Museum, Newport Beach, California. "The Figurative Fifties: New York Figurative Expressionism." July 19–Sept. 18. Traveled to Pennsylvania Academy of the Fine Arts, Philadelphia; Marion Koogler McNay Art Museum, San Antonio, Texas.

1989 Ameringer & Avard Fine Art, Toronto. "Summer Preview."

1990 Brooklyn College of Art.

1991 Whitney Museum of American Art, New York. "Image and Likeness: Figurative Works from the Permanent Collection." Jan. 23–Mar. 20. The Philbrook Museum of Art, Tulsa. "The Landscape in Twentieth-Century American Art: Selections from The Metropolitan Museum of Art." Apr. 14–June 9. Traveled to Center for the Fine Arts, Miami; Joslyn Art Museum, Omaha; Tampa Museum of Art, Florida; Greenville County Museum of Art, South Carolina; Madison Art Center, Wisconsin; Grand Rapids Art Museum, Michigan. The Christian A. Johnson Memorial Gallery, Middlebury College, Middlebury, Vermont. "Fairfield Porter and Rackstraw Downes: The Act of Seeing." May 31–July 7. Miyaga Museum of Art, Sendai, (Miyagi-ken), Japan. "Amerikan, Riarizumu = American Realism & Figurative Art: 1952–1990." Nov. 1–Dec. 23. Traveled to four other Japanese museums.

1992 Maine Coast Artists Gallery, Rockport, Maine. "On the Edge: Forty Years of Maine Painting 1952–1992." Aug. 15–Sept. 27. Traveled to University of Maine at Presque Isle.

SELECTED BIBLIOGRAPHY

Peter Blank

For a relatively complete list of Porter's writings and reviews of Porter's exhibitions as they appear in the periodical literature, consult Rackstraw Downes's bibliography in *Fairfield Porter: Realist Painter in an Age of Abstraction* (1983). *Fairfield Porter: Art In Its Own Terms*, edited by Downes (1979, 1992), is the most complete collection of Porter's writings. Joan Ludman's *Fairfield Porter: A Catalogue Raisonné of His Prints* (1981) contains a bibliography emphasizing literature on Porter's graphic oeuvre. The following bibliography is intended to introduce the reader to the full range of the Porter literature, supplementing these previous bibliographic efforts with additional materials.

Archives and Artists' Files

Freilicher, Jane. Jane Freilicher interviews, Aug. 4 and 5, 1987. Interview of Jane Freilicher conducted by Barbara Shikler for the Archives of American Art. Includes discussion of Porter. Location: Archives of American Art, Washington, D.C.

Gross McCleaf Gallery. Gross McCleaf Gallery artists' files, 1947–1986. Includes materials on Porter, who exhibited at the gallery. Location: Archives of American Art, Washington, D.C.

Hartigan, Grace. Papers, 1942–1969. Includes letters from Porter. Location: George Arents Research Library for Special Collections, Syracuse University, Syracuse, New York.

Hios, Theo. Theo Hios papers, 1938–1981. Includes letters from Porter. Location: Archives of American Art, Washington, D.C.

Hirschl & Adler Galleries. Hirschl & Adler photographs of works of art, [undated] and 1936–1973. Includes: photographs of works of art handled by the Galleries, including Porter. Location: Archives of American Art, Washington, D.C.

Katz, Alex. Alex Katz interview, Oct. 20, 1969. Interview of Katz conducted by Paul Cummings for the Archives of American Art. Includes discussion of Porter. Location: Archives of American Art, Washington, D.C.

Porter, Fairfield. Artists' files. The Museum of Modern Art, New York. Contains miscellaneous exhibition announcements, small catalogs, Museum files.

——————. Artists' files and artists' exhibition files. New York Public Library. Contains miscellaneous exhibition announcements, clippings, catalogues.

——————. Artists' files. Whitney Museum of American Art, New York. Contains miscellaneous exhibition announcements, catalogues.

——————. Interview, June 6, 1968. One sound tape reel; 7 inches (65 p. transcript on one microfilm reel). Interview conducted by Paul Cummings for the Archives of American Art. Location: Archives of American Art, Washington, D.C. Excerpted in *Artists In Their Own Words*, edited by Paul Cummings (1979).

——————. Letter, March, 1976. To Eli Wilentz. From the Wilentz Collection. Location: Poetry and Rare Books Collection, University Libraries, State University of New York at Buffalo.

——————. Papers, 1888–1981. 4.0 linear feet (on 8 microfilm reels). Materials donated by Anne Porter. Materials cover Porter's entire life, his work, friendships, exhibition history, sketchbooks, activities as a critic, correspondence, unpublished materials, etc. Location: Archives of American Art, Washington, D.C.

Stankiewicz, Richard. Richard Stankiewicz papers, 1948–1984. Includes: a 10-page journal, describing a 1955 visit to Fairfield Porter in Maine. Location: Archives of American Art, Washington, D.C.

Wagstaff, Samuel. Samuel Wagstaff papers, 1962–1982. Includes correspondence with Porter. Location: Archives of American Art, Washington, D.C.

Collected Essays, Poetry by the Artist

Porter, Fairfield. *Fairfield Porter: Art in Its Own Terms: Selected Criticism 1935–1975* ; edited and with an introduction by Rackstraw Downes. 1st Zoland ed. Cambridge, Massachusetts: Zoland, 1993. Reprint of the 1979 Taplinger edition. Indexed.

——————. *Fairfield Porter: The Collected Poems With Selected Drawings.* Introduction by John Ashbery; Edited by John Yau with David Kermani. New York: Tibor de Nagy Editions: Promise of Learnings, 1985. ix, 88 p.: ill.; 28 cm.

Books, Catalogue Essays by the Artist

Thomas Eakins. New York: George Braziller, 1959. 127 p.: ill. (some col.); 25 cm. (Great American artists series).

4 Amerikanare: Jasper Johns, Alfred Leslie, Robert Rauschenberg, Richard Stankiewicz. [Stockholm, Sweden: Nationalmuseum. Moderna Museet, 1962]. [100] p.: ill. (50 b&w.); 24 cm. Mar. 17–May 6. Essays by K.G. Hulten, Robert Rosenblum, Andre Parinaud, Fairfield Porter, and Chell. Buffington.

Exhibition of Works by Joseph Cornell. [Pasadena, CA: Pasadena Art Museum, 1966]. [76] p.: ill. (37 b&w.) 18 cm. Dec. 27, 1966–Feb. 11, 1967. Essay by Porter, revised from *Art & Literature*, 8; Spring 1966: 120–130.

American Sculptors and Painters. [Amsterdam: Rijksakademie van Beeldende Kunst, 1968]. [42] p. ill. (21 b&w, 4 col.). Includes chronology and brief biographies. Essay by Porter.

Albert York. [New York: Davis and Langdale Co., Inc., 1982]. [16] p. ill. (9 b&w.); 19 cm. Oct. 12–Nov. 6. Essay by Porter reprinted from Davis Galleries ccatalogue *Albert York: A Loan Exhibition* (1975).

Robert White: A Twenty-five Year Survey Exhibition Bronze and Terra Cotta Figures. [New York: Graham Modern, 1987]. [14] p. ill. (13 b&w, 1 col.). Essays by Valentin Tatransky, Ann Di Pietro, Fairfield Porter, Rhonda Cooper.

Selected Articles by the Artist

"Murals for Workers." *Arise*, 1, 4; April 1935: 21–23.

"Letter to the Editor [on the art criticism of George L.K. Morris and Clement Greenberg]." *Partisan Review*, 8, 1; Jan.–Feb. 1941: 77.

"Reviews and Previews." *Art News*, Dec. 1951–Aug. 1959. Porter composed short reviews of current exhibitions in New York for this section of *Art News*. Concurrent with this reviewing activity he also contributed to the "...Paints a Picture" series.

"Evergood Paints a Picture." *Art News*, 50, 9; Jan. 1952: 30–33, 55–56.

"Rivers Paints a Picture." *Art News*, 52, 9; Jan. 1954: 56–59, 81–83.

"The Nature of John Marin." *Art News*, 54, 1; March 1955: 24–27, 63.

"Letter to the Editor [on Clement Greenberg's definition of American-type painting]." *Partisan Review*, 22, 4; Fall 1955: 570, 572–573. Followed by reply from Greenberg: p. 573.

"Jane Freilicher Paints a Picture." *Art News*, 55, 5; Sept. 1956: 46–49, 65–66.

"David Smith: Steel into Sculpture." *Art News*, 56, 5; Sept. 1957:40–43, 54–55.

"Art." *Nation*, 1959–1961. Porter wrote regularly for the Art section of Nation on various artists and topics within the arts.

"Art [Willem de Kooning]." *Nation*, 188, 23; June 6, 1959: 520–521. Review of de Kooning exhibition at Janis Gallery.

"Art [American abstract painting]." *Nation*, 189, 10; Oct. 3, 1959: 197–199

"Art [representational painting in California, Lucien Day, Nicholas Krushenik]." *Nation*, 189, 21; Dec. 19, 1959: 476.

"Art [Giacometti]." *Nation*, 190, 6; Feb. 6, 1960: 126–127. Review of exhibition at World House Galleries.

"Art [Impressionism and contemporary colorists]." *Nation*, 190, 14; Apr. 2, 1960: 301–302. Includes review of Monet exhibition at The Museum of Modern Art, New York.

"Art [Edwin Dickinson, Rothko, Richenburg]." *Nation*, 192, 8; Feb. 25, 1961: 175–176.

"Art [14th–18th century Italian drawings, French art from 1600–1750]." *Nation*, 192, 14; April 8, 1961: 309–311. Both exhibitions at The Metropolitan Museum of Art, New York.

"Art [American painting 1865–1905]." *Nation*, 192, 23; June 10, 1961: 506–507. Exhibition at Whitney Museum of American Art.

"Class content in American Abstract Painting." *Art News*, 61, 2; April 1962: 26–28, 48–49.

"The Education of Jasper Johns." *Art News*, 62, 10; Feb. 1964: 44–45, 61–62.

"Metropolitan Museum: Ban the Megamuseum." *Art News*, 68, 9; Jan. 1970: 59–60.

"Speaking Likeness." *Art News Annual*, 36; 1970: 40–51. Issue titled *Narrative Art*. Excerpted as "Art and Scientific Method" in *Art In Its Own Terms*.

"Letter to the editor [Nuclear power plants : the principal objection]." *The New York Times*, Jan. 31, 1974: 32.

Books about the Artist

Ludman, Joan. *Fairfield Porter: A Catalogue Raisonné of His Prints, Including Illustrations, Bookjackets, and Exhibition Posters*. Westbury, New York: Highland House, c. 1981. 160 p.: ill. (some col.); 29 cm. Bibliography: p. 148–154.

Spike, John T. *Fairfield Porter, An American Classic*. Checklist of the paintings of Fairfield Porter by Joan Ludman. New York: Abrams, 1992. 320 p.: ill. (some col.); 27 cm. Includes bibliographical references and index.

Articles, Selected Reviews, Interviews, Essays about the Artist

Devree, Howard. "In the Galleries." *The New York Times*, May 14, 1933: X, 8. Review of 1933 dual exhibition with Simeon Braguin at offices of Theodore A. Kohn & Son.

Preston, Stuart. "Chiefly Modern." *The New York Times*, Oct. 12, 1952: II, 9. Includes "Intimist: Review of 1952 de Nagy Exhibition."

Campbell, Lawrence. "Reviews and Previews." *Art News*, 51, 6; Oct. 1952: 45. Review of 1952 de Nagy exhibition.

Fitzsimmons, James. "Fifty-Seventh Street in Review." *Art Digest*, 27, 3; Nov. 1, 1952: 19–20. Review of 1952 de Nagy exhibition.

O'Hara, Frank. "Reviews and Previews." *Art News*, 53, 2; April 1954: 46.

Review of 1954 de Nagy exhibition.

Ashton, Dore. "Fortnight in Review." *Art Digest*, 28, 15; May 1, 1954: 16. Review of 1954 de Nagy exhibition.

O'Hara, Frank. "Porter Paints a Picture." *Art News*, 53, 9; Jan. 1955: 38–41, 66–67. Portrait of Katharine Porter.

Campbell, Lawrence. "Reviews and Previews." *Art News*, 54, 1; March 1955: 49. Review of 1955 de Nagy exhibition.

Hess, Thomas B. "United States Painting: Some Recent Directions." *Art News Annual*, 25; 1956: 73–98, 174.

"Selecting from the Flow of Spring Shows." *Art News*, 55, 2; April 1956: 24–27. "An Almost Naive Literalness"/ Parker Tyler: 26–27. Review of 1956 de Nagy exhibition.

Schuyler, James. "Reviews and Previews." *Art News*, 57, 3; May 1958: 13. Review of 1958 de Nagy exhibition.

Tillim, Sidney. "In the Galleries." *Arts*, 33, 6; March 1959: 56. Review of 1959 de Nagy exhibition.

Tillim, Sidney. "Month in Review." *Arts*, 35, 3; Dec. 1960: 45–46. Review of 1960 de Nagy exhibition.

Tillim, Sidney. "In the Galleries." *Arts*, 36, 5; Feb. 1962: 38. Review of 1962 de Nagy exhibition.

Kramer, Hilton. "New York: Season's Gleanings." *Art in America*, 51, 3; June 1963: 131–136. "The Duality of Fairfield Porter": 134. Review of 1963 de Nagy exhibition.

"The Human Figure Returns in Separate Ways and Places." *Life*, 52, 23; June 8, 1962: 54–61. Comparison of East and West Coast figurative artists (Diebenkorn, Bischoff, Park, Wonner, Porter, Katz, Dodd, Marcus).

Benedikt, Michael. "Fairfield Porter: Minimum of Melodrama." *Art News*, 63, 1; March 1964: 36–37, 66–67. Review of 1964 de Nagy exhibition.

O'Doherty, Brian. "Art: By Fairfield Porter: His School of Paris Works, Which Bring the Outdoors In, Shown at de Nagy's." *The New York Times*, March 24, 1964: 32.

Lanes, Jerrold. "Fairfield Porter's Recent Work." *Arts*, 38, 7; April 1964: 40–43. Review of 1964 de Nagy exhibition. For reply by Porter and rejoinder by Lanes see *Arts*, 39, 1; Oct. 1964: 6.

Kramer, Hilton. "Fairfield Porter: Against the Historical Grain." *The New York Times*, Feb. 20, 1966: II, 17.

Schuyler, James. "Immediacy is the Message: Fairfield Porter's New Works." *Art News*, 66, 1; Mar. 1967: 32–33, 68–70. Review of 1967 de Nagy exhibition.

Kramer, Hilton. "An Art of Conservation." *The New York Times*, Feb. 9, 1969: 33.

Mellow, James R. "New York Letter." *Art International*, 13, 3; March 20, 1969: 56–60. Review of 1969 de Nagy exhibition: 57.

Campbell, Lawrence. "Reviews and Previews." *Art News*, 69, 2; April 1970: 71. Review of 1970 de Nagy exhibition.

Henning, Edward B. "South of His House, North of His House: Nyack, A Painting by Fairfield Porter." *Bulletin of The Cleveland Museum of Art*, 53, 3; Mar. 1971: 85–90.

Cummings, Paul. "Fairfield Porter." *Archives of American Art Journal*, 12, 2; 1972: 10–21. Excerpted from the 1968 interview conducted by Cummings. See Archives section. Transcription varies slightly from *Artists in Their Own Words* / Cummings (1979).

Kramer, Hilton. "Art." *The New York Times*, March 9, 1974: 25. Review of 1974 de Nagy exhibition.

Campbell, Lawrence. "Reviews and Previews." *Art News*, 73, 5; May 1974: 102. Review of Hirschl & Adler 1974 exhibition.

Shirey, David. "Porter's Works on Display." *The New York Times*, Dec. 22, 1974: 64. Review of 1974 Heckscher retrospective.

Downes, Rackstraw. "What the Sixties Meant to Me." *Art Journal*, 34, 2; Winter 1974/75: 125–131.

Hess, Thomas B. "Fairfield Porter." *New York*, 8, 51; Dec. 22, 1975: 82. Review of 1975 Brooke Alexander watercolor exhibition and comparison of Porter with Arthur Dove.

Myers, John Bernard. "Fairfield Porter 1907–1975." *Parenthèse*, 3; 1975.

"Four Tributes." *Art in America*, 64, 1; Jan.–Feb. 1976: 20. Fairfield Porter 1907–75 / John Ashbery. Obituary.

De Mott, Benjamin. "Unified Man: Ground Floor" *Atlantic*, 237, 4; April 1976: 110. Obituary and reminiscence in Culture Watch section.

Kramer, Hilton. "Chase, Porter, and History." *The New York Times*, May 14, 1976: III, 15. Review of 1976 Hirschl & Adler exhibition.

Finkelstein, Louis. "The Naturalness of Fairfield Porter." *Arts Magazine*, 50, 9; May 1976: 102–105.

Kramer, Hilton. "Why Figurative Art Confounds our Museums." *The New York Times*, Jan. 2, 1977: II, 19.

Downes, Rackstraw. "Fairfield Porter: The Painter as Critic." *Art Journal*, 37, 4; Summer 1978: 306–312. Reprinted as introduction in *Fairfield Porter: Art In Its Own Terms* (1979).

Sandler, Irving. *The New York School: The Painters and Sculptors of the Fifties*. New York: Harper & Row, 1978. 366 p.: ill. (8 col.); 26 cm. Porter is discussed as a "gestural realist."

Cummings, Paul. *Artists In Their Own Words*. New York: St. Martin's Press, 1979. 242 p.: ill.; 22 cm. Includes excerpts from Cumming's 1968 interview for the Archives of American Art. Transcription varies slightly from Cummings, *Archives of American Art Journal*, 12, 2; 1972.

Schjeldahl, Peter. [Review of *Art In Its Own Terms*]. *Portfolio*, 1, 2; June-July 1979: 77–78.

Beem, E.A. "People and Things Connected: Fairfield Porter, Creator and Critic." *Portland Independent*, July 27, 1979. Review of Barridoff Galleries 1979 exhibition.

Doudera, Gerard. "The Wholeness of Fairfield Porter's Vision." *Bulletin of the William Benton Museum of Art*, 1, 7; 1979: 15–27.

Kramer, Hilton. "Fairfield Porter: A Virtuoso Colorist." *The New York Times*, Nov. 25, 1979: II, 23, 32. Review of Hirschl & Adler 1979 exhibition.

Sutton, Denys. "The painter as critic." *Apollo*, 114, 234; Aug. 1981: 74–75. Review of *Art In Its Own Terms*.

Henry, Gerrit. "Painterly Realism and the Modern Landscape." *Art in America*, 69, 7; Sept. 1981: 112–119.

Myers, John Bernard. "Fairfield Porter: Poet of the Commonplace." *Portfolio*, 5, 1; Jan.-Feb. 1983: 54–61. Review of 1983 Boston retrospective.

Balliett, Whitney. "An Akimbo Quality." *The New Yorker*, Mar. 14, 1983: 140, 143–147. Review of 1983 Boston retrospective.

Downes, Rackstraw. "Fairfield Porter's Unrepeatable Days." *Art News*. 82, 4; Apr. 1983: 94–99. Review of 1983 Boston retrospective.

Kramer, Hilton. "Fairfield Porter: An American Classic." *New Criterion*, 1, 9; May 1983: 1–7. Review of 1983 Boston retrospective.

Berlind, Robert. "Fairfield Porter: Natural Premises." *Art in America*, 71, 8; Sept. 1983: 136–143. Review of 1983 Boston retrospective.

MacLeod, Glen. "Fairfield Porter and Wallace Stevens : Kindred Spirits of American Art." *Archives of American Art Journal*, 24, 1; 1984: 2–12.

Lyons, Lisa, and Robert Storr. *Chuck Close*. New York: Rizzoli, 1987. 184 p.: ill. (some col.); 34 cm. Essay by Storr discusses Close's realism in the context of his contemporaries, especially Porter, Katz, and Pearlstein.

——————. *Spirit of Place: Contemporary Landscape Painting and the American Tradition*. Boston: Bulfinch Press, c. 1989. 159 p.: ill. (some col.); 28 cm. "Selected Bibliography": p. 159. Includes discussion of and works by Porter.

Updike, John. "Violence at the Windows." In *Just looking*. New York: Alfred A. Knopf, 1989. 210 p. ill. (some col.); 24 cm. Reprinted from *New Republic*, 188, 3554; Feb. 28, 1983: 24–25. Review of 1983 Boston retrospective.

Ward, John L. *American Realist Painting, 1945–1980*. Ann Arbor. Michigan: UMI Research Press, c. 1989. (Studies in the Fine Arts. The Avant-garde; no. 60). 431 p.: ill.; 24 cm. Bibliography: p. 391–420. Includes discussion of and works by Porter.

Shapiro, David. "Fairfield Porter's Quiet Revolution." *Art & Antiques*, n.s., 7, 3; Mar. 1990: 110–115, 166–168.

Kirwin, Liza. "Visual Thinking: Sketchbooks from the Archives of American Art." *Archives of American Art Journal*, 30, 1–4; 1990: 155–163. Reprinted from *Archives of American Art Journal*, 27, 1; 1987: 21–29.

Kramer, Hilton. "Fairfield Porter at Hunter: A Master Long Ignored." *The New York Observer*, Apr. 20, 1992: 1, 23. Review of 1992 Bertha and Karl Leubsdorf Art Gallery, Hunter College exhibition.

Exhibition Catalogs—One and Two-Person Shows
(arranged chronologically)

Fairfield Porter: Paintings. New York: Tibor de Nagy Gallery, 1963. [4] p.: one ill.; 21 cm. Jan. 29–Feb. 16, 1963.

Fairfield Porter: Paintings. New York: Tibor de Nagy Gallery, 1964. 1 folded sheet ([4] p.): 1 ill.; 19 cm. Mar. 17–Apr. 11, 1964.

Fairfield Porter, Paintings. Carbondale: The University, [1964]. 1 v. (unpaged). Nov. 1–27, 1964. Mr. and Mrs. John Russell Mitchell Gallery, Southern Illinois University.

Fairfield Porter: Paintings. [New York: The Gallery, 1965]. [4] p.: 3 ill.; 21 cm. Tibor de Nagy, Feb. 16–Mar. 25, 1965.

Fairfield Porter: Recent Paintings. [New York: The Gallery, 1966]. one folded sheet ([6] p.): 4 ill.; 21 cm. Tibor de Nagy Gallery, Feb. 15–Mar. 5, 1966.

Fairfield Porter: Recent Paintings. New York: The Gallery, 1967. one folded sheet ([6] p.): 4 ill.; 21 cm. Tibor de Nagy Gallery, Feb. 18–Mar. 16, 1967.

Fairfield Porter, Paintings; Eliot Porter, Photographs. Waterville, Maine: The Museum, [1969]. [17] p.: ill.; 23 cm. Colby College Art Museum, May 6–June 24, 1969. Catalogue prepared by James M. Carpenter.

Recent Work by Fairfield Porter. New York : Hirschl and Adler Galleries, [1972]. [16] p.: ill. (9 b&w, 1 col.); 16 x 23 cm. Apr. 11–29, 1972. Includes chronology. Forward by Peter Schjeldahl. 48 works.

An Exhibition of Paintings by Fairfield Porter. [Baltimore: The Maryland Institute, College of Art, Mount Royal Station Gallery, 1972]. [6] p.: 1 ill.; 21 cm. Oct. 20–Nov. 18, 1972. Essay by Eugene Leake. 54 works, primarily from Hirschl & Adler Galleries.

Fairfield Porter. [Cold Spring Harbor, New York : Harbor Gallery, 1973]. [4] p.: ill. (7 b&w.); 14 cm. Aug. 19–Sept. 15, 1973. 32 works.

Recent Work by Fairfield Porter. [New York: Hirschl and Adler Galleries, 1974]. [13] p.: ill. (9 b&w, 1 col.). Mar. 2–23, 1974. Includes statement by the artist, biography. 46 works.

Fairfield Porter: Retrospective Exhibition. [Huntington, New York: The Heckscher Museum, 1974]. [14] p. ill. (12 b&w, 1 col.). The Heckscher Museum, Huntington, New York, Dec. 15, 1974–Jan. 26, 1975, and two other locations. Includes chronology. Essay by Eva Ingersoll Gatling. 69 works.

Fairfield Porter: Paintings 1955–1975. Storrs, Connecticut: University of Connecticut, 1975. i folded sheet ([4] p.): ill.; 23 cm. Essay by Gerard Doudera.

Fairfield Porter: His Last Works 1974–1975. New York: Hirschl & Adler

Galleries, [1976]. [12] p.: ill. (2 col.); 21 cm. May 4–28, 1976. Biography. Brief essay by Prescott D. Schutz. 50 works.

Fairfield Porter (1907–1976). [Cold Spring Harbor, New York: Harbor Gallery, 1977]. [8] p. ill. (5 b&w, 1 col.). Mar. 13–Apr. 16, 1977. Essay by Claire Nicolas White. 30 works.

Fairfield Porter's Maine. Southampton, New York: The Parrish Art Museum, [1977]. [8] p.; ill., port.: 23 cm. July 2–Sept. 11, 1977, and one other location. Essay by Helen Harrison. 43 works.

Fairfield Porter: His Last Works: 1974–1975. [Los Angeles, California: Esther-Robles Gallery, 1978]. [6] p. ill. (4 b&w.). Oct. 3–27, 1978. Essay by Prescott Schutz and biography from Hirschl & Adler *Last Works* exhibition (1976). 20 works.

Fairfield Porter. Portland, Maine: Barridoff Galleries, 1979. July 23–Sept. 3. Essay by Rackstraw Downes.

Fairfield Porter: Figurative Painting. New York: [The Galleries, 1979]. [12] p.: chiefly ill. (some col.); 21 cm. Hirschl & Adler Gallery, Nov. 3–Dec. 1, 1979. Essay by Prescott D. Schutz. Biography. 35 works.

Prints by Fairfield Porter. Southampton: The Museum, [1982]. 8 p.; ill.: 21 cm. The Parrish Art Museum, Apr. 18–June 6, 1982. From the Lauris and Daniel J. Mason Collection. Essay by Joan Ludman excerpted from her 1981 print catalogue raisonné essay. 14 prints.

Fairfield Porter (1907–1975): Realist Painter in an Age of Abstraction. Essays by John Ashbery and Kenworth Moffett; contributions by John Bernard Myers, Paul Cummings, Prescott D. Schutz, Rackstraw Downes, and Louise Hamlin. Boston: Museum of Fine Arts, c. 1983. 107 p.: ill. (31 b&w, 30 col.), ports.; 29 cm. Museum of Fine Arts, Boston, Jan. 12–Mar. 13, 1983, and four other locations. Bibliography: p. 97–101. Includes chronology, poetry by Porter, and excerpts from the Cummings interview.

Fairfield Porter: Whitney Museum of American Art, New York. New York: The Museum, 1984. one folded sheet ([6] p.): ill. (2 col.), port.; 23 cm. June 1–Aug. 19, 1984. Flyer for the 1983 retrospective which originated from Boston.

Fairfield Porter: Portraits. New York: Whitney Museum of American Art, 1984. [8] p.: ill. (col. cov.); 21 cm. June 8–Aug. 22, 1984, Whitney Museum of American Art, Fairfield County, Stamford, Connecticut. Essay by Pamela Gruninger. Includes statements by portraits' subjects. 37 works.

Fairfield Porter: Paintings and Works on Paper. [Chicago: The Club, 1984]. [16] p.: chiefly ill. (some col.), port.; 26 cm. Arts Club of Chicago, Nov. 12–Dec. 31, 1984. 44 works drawn primarily from Hirschl & Adler Modern. Catalogue includes an essay by Eliot Porter, "My Brother Fairfield," and excerpts from an article by Rackstraw Downes, reprinted from *Art News*, 82, 4; Apr. 1983.

Fairfield Porter, 1907–1975. New York: Hirschl & Adler Modern, [1985]. [40] p.: ill. (4 b&w, 15 col.), ports.; 27 cm. Sept. 5–28, 1985. Includes poem ("The Mountain") and statement from Hirschl & Adler 1974 exhibition. Includes solo and group exhibition chronology. 43 paintings, 20 works on paper.

Fairfield Porter: The Late Watercolors. Prescott D. Schutz, guest curator. Katonah, New York: The Gallery, c. 1986. [20] p.: ill. (8 b&w.); 21 cm. Katonah Gallery, June 15–Aug. 10, 1986, and two other locations. Includes biography. Essay by Schutz. 35 works.

Fairfield Porter and Rackstraw Downes: The Act of Seeing. [Middlebury, Vermont: The Christian A. Johnson Memorial Gallery, Middlebury College, 1991]. [5] leaves (fold.); ill. (5 col.); 25 cm. May 31–July 7, 1991. Introduction by Emmie Donadio, excerpts from interview by Donadio with Downes. Folded brochure includes insert of interview by Donadio with Downes: A Conversation with Rackstraw Downes. 14 p.; 23 cm.

Porter Pairings: A Selection of Works by Fairfield Porter from The Parrish Art Museum, Southampton/William C. Agee with Malama Maron-Bersin, Sara Rosenfeld, and Michele White. [New York]: Bertha and Karl Leubsdorf Art Gallery, Hunter College of The City University of New York, 1992. 47 p.: ill. (some col.); 22 cm. Mar. 31–May 22, 1992. Includes bibliographic references.

Fairfield Porter: An American Painter. [Southampton, New York: The Parrish Art Museum, 1993]. The Parrish Art Museum, June 26– Sept. 12, 1993, and five other locations. Essay by William C. Agee. Includes chronology, exhibitions listing, bibliography.

Exhibition Catalogues—Group Shows
(arranged chronologically)

1959 Annual Exhibition of Contemporary American Painting. New York: Whitney Museum of American Art, 1959. [20] p.: ill. (28 b&w.). Dec. 9, 1959–Jan. 31, 1960.

Annual Exhibition, 1961: Contemporary American Painting. New York: Whitney Museum of American Art, 1961. [62] p.: ill (63 b&w.). Dec. 13, 1961–Feb. 4, 1962.

Annual Exhibition, 1963: Contemporary American Painting. New York: Whitney Museum of American Art, 1963. [63] p.: ill. (18 b&w.). Dec. 11, 1963–Feb. 2, 1964.

1965 Annual Exhibition: Contemporary American Painting. New York: Whitney Museum of American Art, 1965. [62] p.: ill. (60 b&w.). Dec. 8, 1965– Jan. 30, 1966.

1967 Annual Exhibition of Contemporary Painting. New York: Whitney Museum of American Art, 1967. [76] p.: ill. (63 b&w.). Dec. 13, 1967– Feb. 4, 1968.

Venice 34: The Figurative Tradition in Recent American Art / by Norman A. Geske. Washington, D.C.: Smithsonian Institution Press, [1968]. 131 p.: ill. (60 b&w., 10 col.); 27 cm. Prepared for the 34th Venice Biennial. United States Pavilion, Venice, Italy, June 22–Oct. 20, 1968, and two other locations. Essay by Geske. Works by Baskin, Burford, Cremean, Dickinson, Diebenkorn, Gallo, Grooms, McGarrell, Nakian, and Porter.

Painterly Realism. [New York: American Federation of Arts, 1970]. one vol. (unpaged): ill.; 26 cm. Exhibition of 47 artists held at Smith College Museum of Art, Northampton, Massachusetts. Essay by Michael Wentworth. Bill Sullivan consultant and selector.

Lithographs by de Kooning, Fairfield Porter, Paul Waldman. New York: M. Knoedler & Co., [1972]. [16] p.: ill. (23 b&w.); 22 cm. Five lithographs from 1970–71, printed at Bank Street Atelier. No essay.

The Artists of Suffolk County: Part VI: Contemporary Prints. Huntington,New York: The Heckscher Museum, 1972. July 16–Sept. 3.

Aspects of the Figure. Cleveland: The Cleveland Museum of Art, 1974. 40 p.: ill.; 23 cm. July 10–Sept. 1, 1974. Works by Beal, Beckman, Bruder, Clarke, Hall, Hickam, Hsai, Lee-Smith, McLean, Midgette, Pearlstein, Perlis, Schonzeit, Soyer, Thiebaud, and Porter. Introduction by Edward B. Henning.

New York, New York. New York: Associated American Artists, 1974. [4] p. Aug. 5–30.

Candid Painting: American Genre 1950-1975. [Lincoln, Massachusetts]: De Cordova Museum Press, 1975. [36] p.: ill. (32 b.&w.); 31 cm. Oct. 12– Dec. 7, 1975. Essay by Eva Jacob. Works by Beal, Dash, Elaine de Kooning, Freilicher, Georges, Rivers, Soyer, Porter (four), and 22 others.

America 1976: A Bicentennial Exhibition Sponsored by the United States Department of the Interior. [Washington, D.C.]: Hereward Lester Cooke Foundation, 1976. 116 p.: ill. (38 b&w., 57 col.); 24 x 27 cm. Corcoran Gallery of Art, Washington, D.C., Apr. 27–June 6, 1976, and eight other locations. Works commissioned by Department of Interior. Essays by John Ashbery, Neil Welliver, and Richard Howard.

Artists of Suffolk County: Part X: Recorders of History. Huntington, New York: The Heckscher Museum, 1976. 24 p.; ill. (16 b&w.). May 9–June 20. Introduction by Ruth Solomon.

Selections from the Lawrence H. Bloedel Bequest and Related Works from the Permanent Collection of the Whitney Museum of American Art. New York: The Museum, 1977. 55 p.: ill.; 26 cm. Apr. 5–June 19.

New York on Paper. New York: Whitney Museum of American Art, 1977. [4] p.: ill.; 23 cm. Apr. 7–May 22. Selected prints and drawings from the Museum's collection.

Catalog, 25th National Exhibition of Prints. Washington, D.C.: Library of Congress, 1977. [14] p.: ill.; 26 x 20 cm. May 27–Sept. 18. Biennial National Exhibition of Prints held at National Collection of Fine Arts and circulated as traveling exhibition.

Two Decades of American Printmaking, 1957–1977. Worcester, Massachusetts: Worcester Art Museum, 1978. 27 p.: ill.; 23 cm. Mar. 15–May 14. Drawn from the museum's collection.

In Celebration: Selections from the Private Collection of Roy R. and Marie S. Neuberger, Neuberger Museum, State University of New York ... Purchase. Purchase: The Museum, 1978. [48] p.: ill. (40 b&w, 1 col.); 21 cm. Sept. 24–Nov. 26.

The Porter Family. Southampton, New York: The Museum, [c. 1980]. 23 p.: ill. (col. cover); 22 cm. The Parrish Art Museum, May 18–July 13, 1980. Works by Aline, Eliot, Fairfield, and Stephen Porter. Essay by Philip Ferrato. 79 total works (18 by Fairfield Porter). Includes bibliographical references.

The Figurative Tradition and the Whitney Museum of American Art: Painting and Sculpture from the Permanent Collection/by Patricia Hills and Roberta K. Tarbell. New York: The Museum, 1980. 191 p.: ill. (some col.); 28 cm. June 25–Sept. 28, 1980. Essays by Tarbell and Hills. Bibliography: p. 183–184. Includes one work by Porter in an exhibition of 151 artists.

Realism, Photo-Realism. Tulsa, Oklahoma: Philbrook Art Center, 1980. 123 p.; ill. (30 col.): 29 cm. Philbrook Art Center, Oct. 5–Nov. 23, 1980. Essay, catalogue, and selections by John Arthur. One painting and one work on paper each by 30 American artists.

American Figure Painting: 1950–1980. Norfolk, Virginia: The Chrysler Museum, 1980. 116 p.: ill. (some col.); 27 cm. Oct. 17–Nov. 30, 1980. Essay by Thomas W. Styron. One work each by 86 artists.

Realism and Realities: The Other Side of American Painting 1940–1960. New Brunswick, New Jersey: Rutgers University Art Gallery, 1981. 195 p.: ill. (some col.); 31 cm. Rutgers University Art Gallery, Jan. 17–Mar. 26, 1981, and two other locations. Essays by Greta Berman and Jeffrey Wechsler. Includes 162 works, one by Porter.

Real, Really Real, Super Real: Directions in Contemporary American Realism/ organized by the San Antonio Museum Association. San Antonio, Texas: The Association, c. 1981. 200 p.: ill. (some col.); 31 cm. San Antonio Museum of Art, Mar. 1–Apr. 26, 1981, and four other locations. Essays by Alvin Martin, Linda Nochlin, Philip Pearlstein. Bibliography: p. 195–196. 59 works by 58 artists.

The Contemporary American Landscape. New York: The Gallery, [1981]. [32] p.: ill. (some col.); 25 cm. Hirschl & Adler Contemporaries, May 2–29, 1981. Essay by Frank H. Goodyear, Jr. Included four works by Porter in an exhibition of 39 works by 13 artists.

Contemporary American Realism Since 1960/Frank H. Goodyear, Jr. Boston: New York Graphic Society in association with the Pennsylvania Academy of the Fine Arts, c. 1981. 255 p.: ill. (some col.); 29 cm. Pennsylvania Academy of the Fine Arts, Sept. 18–Dec. 13, 1981, and two other locations, plus Portugal and Germany. Essay by Goodyear. Bibliography: p. 233–242.

Art and Friendship: A Tribute to Fairfield Porter/Helen A. Harrison, Prescott D. Schutz, co-curators. East Hampton, New York: Guild Hall Museum, 1984. 12 p.: ill.; 21 cm. Guild Hall Museum, Apr. 14–June 3, 1984, and two other locations. Includes works by fifteen painters: Blaine, Button, Dash, Elaine de Kooning, Willem de Kooning, Downes, Freilicher, Georges, Grooms, Katz, Leake, Rivers, Welliver, Wilson, York; one work by Porter.

Painting Naturally: Fairfield Porter & His Influences. Southampton, New York: The Museum, c. 1984. [24] p.: ill.; 21 cm. The Parrish Art Museum, Apr. 15–June 3, 1984. Essay by Klaus Kertess. Includes 16 works by other artists such as Bonnard, Vuillard, Willem de Kooning, Kline, Marin, Rivers, and Freilicher, and 20 works by Porter.

American Realism: Twentieth-Century Drawings and Watercolors from the Glenn C. Janss Collection. San Francisco: San Francisco Museum of Modern Art, 1986. 240 p.: ill. (some col.); 25 cm. Essay by Alvin Martin.

Still Life: Painting Sculpture Drawing. [Manitowoc, Wisconsin: Rahr West Art Museum, 1987]. [16] p.: 13 col. ill.; 18 cm. July 26–Sept. 6, 1987. Essay by John Post Lee. One work each by twenty-seven artists, including Avery, Dickinson, Buston, Krasner, Neel, Park, Thiebaud, Wilson, Butler, and Porter.

The Figurative Fifties: New York Figurative Expressionism/organized by Paul Schimmel ... and Judith E. Stein. Newport Beach, California: Newport Harbor Art Museum, [1988]. 195 p.: ill. (some col.); 26 cm. Newport Harbor Art Museum, July 19–Sept. 18, 1988, and two other locations. General essays by Klaus Kertess, Carter Ratcliff, Schimmel, and Stein, with individudal essays on 13 artists; Porter essay by Brian O'Doherty. Ten of the 81 works by Porter.

Image and Likeness: Figurative Works from the Permanent Collection of the Whitney Museum of American Art. [New York: The Museum, 1991]. 16 p.; ill.: 25 cm. Whitney Museum, Downtown at Federal Reserve Plaza, Jan. 23–Mar. 20, and one other location. Exhibition from permanent collection dating from 1952–82.

The Landscape in Twentieth-Century American Art: Selections from The Metropolitan Museum of Art/introduction by Robert Rosenblum; catalogue texts by Lowery Stokes Sims and Lisa M. Messinger. New York: Rizzoli International Publications; American Federation of Arts, 1991. 174 p.: ill. (some col.); 26 cm. Opened at Philbrook Museum of Art, Tulsa, Apr. 14–June 9, 1991, and traveled to six other locations. Bibliographic notes. Works by 60 artists.

Amerikan, Riarizumu=American Realism & Figurative Art: 1952–1990. [Sendai-Shi]: Miyagi-Ken Bijutsukan, 1991. 215 p.; col. ill.: 28 cm. Miyaga Museum of Art, Sendai, Japan, Nov. 1–Dec. 23, 1991, and four other Japanese museums. Essay by John Arthur.

On The Edge: Forty Years of Maine Painting 1952–1992. Rockport, Maine: Maine Coast Artists, 1992. 168 p.: ill. (some col.); 21 cm. Maine Coast Artists Gallery, Aug. 15–Sept. 27, 1992, and one other location. Essay by Theodore Wolff. Works by 104 artists.

CHECKLIST OF THE EXHIBITION

1. *Seated Boy*. c. 1938.
    Oil on Masonite, 18 x 14 in.
    The Parrish Art Museum,
    Gift of the Estate of Fairfield Porter

2. *Cityscape*. c. 1945.
    Oil on Masonite, 25 x 30 in.
    The Parrish Art Museum,
    Gift of Robert Fizdale, in Memory of Arthur Gold

3. *Wildflowers*. c. 1948.
    Oil on Masonite, 17 x 13 1/2 in.
    The Parrish Art Museum,
    Gift of the Estate of Fairfield Porter

4. *Chair*. c. 1949.
    Oil on Masonite, 16 x 11 7/8 in.
    The Parrish Art Museum,
    Gift of the Estate of Fairfield Porter

5. *Painting Materials*. c. 1949.
    Oil on canvas, 32 1/8 x 25 1/8 in.
    The Parrish Art Museum,
    Gift of the Estate of Fairfield Porter

6. *Studio Interior*. 1951.
    Oil on canvas, 36 x 42 in.
    Courtesy Mickelson Gallery, Washington, D.C.

7. *Laurence Typing*. 1952.
    Oil on canvas, 40 x 30 1/8 in.
    The Parrish Art Museum,
    Gift of the Estate of Fairfield Porter

8. *Katie and Jacob in the Yard*. c. 1953.
    Oil on canvas, 41 1/2 x 44 in.
    Collection Katherine Koch, Brooklyn, New York

9. *Lawn Scene*. 1953.
    Oil on canvas, 41 1/2 x 44 in.
    The Parrish Art Museum, Littlejohn Collection

10. *Lunch under the Elm Tree*. 1954.
    Oil on canvas, 78 x 60 1/4 in.
    The Parrish Art Museum,
    Gift of the Estate of Fairfield Porter

11. *Armchair on Porch*. 1955.
    Oil on canvas, 37 1/8 x 45 in.
    Collection Dr. Marianne de Nagy Buchenhorner,
    Courtesy Tibor de Nagy Gallery, New York

12. *Katie and Anne*. 1955.
    Oil on canvas, 80 1/8 x 62 1/8 in.
    Hirshhorn Museum and Sculpture Garden,
    Smithsonian Institution, Washington, D.C.,
    Gift of Joseph Hirshhorn, 1966

13. *Trail*. c. 1955.
    Oil on Masonite, 15 x 15 1/8 in.
    The Parrish Art Museum,
    Gift of the Estate of Fairfield Porter

14. *Portrait of Elaine de Kooning*. 1957.
    Oil on canvas, 62 x 41 in.
    The Metropolitan Museum of Art, New York,
    Gift of Mrs. Fairfield Porter, 1978.

15. *Still Life*. 1958.
    Oil on canvas, 39 x 30 1/2 in.
    Collection The Equitable Life Assurance
    Society of the U.S.

16. *Chrysanthemums*. 1958.
    Oil on canvas, 40 x 32 in.
    Wadsworth Atheneum, Hartford, Connecticut,
    The Ella Gallup Sumner and Mary Catlin Sumner
    Collection

17. *Anne, Lizzie, and Katie*. 1958.
    Oil on canvas, 78 x 60 in.
    Sheldon Memorial Art Gallery,
    University of Nebraska—Lincoln, Nebraska
    Art Association, Thomas C. Woods Memorial
    Collection, 1962

18. *A. K. J.* 1959.
    Oil on canvas, 36 x 48 in.
    Private Collection, New York

19. *East 11th Street*. c. 1960.
    Oil on canvas, 29 7/8 x 23 7/8 in.
    The Parrish Art Museum,
    Gift of the Estate of Fairfield Porter

20. *Lizzie with Wild Roses*. 1960.
Oil on canvas, 30 1/8 x 20 1/8 in.
The Parrish Art Museum,
Gift of the Estate of Fairfield Porter

21. *Calm Morning*. 1961.
Oil on canvas, 36 x 36 in.
Collection Arthur M. Bullowa, New York

22. *Rocking Horse*. 1962.
Oil on canvas, 36 x 36 in.
Collection Mr. and Mrs. Donald Newhouse, New
York

23. *Primroses*. c. 1963.
Oil on canvas, 30 x 24 in.
The Parrish Art Museum,
Gift of the Estate of Fairfield Porter

24. *Short Walk*. 1963.
Oil on canvas, 62 x 47 3/4 in.
Collection Jane L. Richards, New York

25. *The Screen Porch*. 1964.
79 1/2 x 79 1/2 in.
Whitney Museum of American Art, New York,
Lawrence H. Bloedel Bequest

26. *July Interior*. 1964.
Oil on canvas, 56 x 72 in.
Hirshhorn Museum and Sculpture Garden,
Smithsonian Institution, Washington, D.C.,
Gift of Joseph Hirshhorn, 1966

27. *Six O'Clock*. 1964.
Oil on canvas, 71 1/4 x 59 1/2 in.
The Saint Louis Art Museum, Missouri,
Gift of Mr. and Mrs. B. Crosby Kemper, Jr.,
through The Crosby Kemper Foundations
(not in exhibition)

28. *Still Life with Standing Figure*. 1964.
Oil on canvas, 45 x 45 in.
Collection Jane P. Norman, New York

29. *The Living Room*. 1964.
Oil on canvas, 60 x 48 in.
Collection Constance Jewett Ellis, New York

30. *Morning Landscape*. 1965.
Oil on canvas, 79 1/2 x 80 in.
Santa Barbara Museum of Art, Gift of Mrs. Rowe
Giesen, in celebration of the museum's 50th
anniversary

31. *Anne*. 1965.
Oil on canvas, 47 x 28 in.
The Parrish Art Museum,
Gift of the Estate of Fairfield Porter

32. *The Mirror*. 1966.
Oil on canvas, 72 x 60 in.
The Nelson-Atkins Museum of Art, Kansas
City, Missouri, Gift of the Enid and
Crosby Kemper Foundation

33. *Early Morning*. 1966.
Oil on canvas, 32 x 28 in.
Collection Douglas and Beverly Feurring,
Boca Raton, Florida

34. *Penobscot Bay with Peak Island*. 1966.
Oil on canvas, 48 x 59 1/8 in.
The Parrish Art Museum,
Gift of the Estate of Fairfield Porter

35. *Nyack*. 1966-67.
Oil on canvas, 82 x 110 in.
Contemporary Collection of The Cleveland
Museum of Art, Ohio

36. *View towards the Studio*. 1967.
Oil on canvas, 39 x 25 1/8 in.
The Parrish Art Museum,
Gift of the Estate of Fairfield Porter

37. *Anne in a Striped Dress*. 1967.
Oil on canvas, 55 x 48 in.
The Parrish Art Museum,
Gift of the Estate of Fairfield Porter

38. *Jane and Elizabeth*. 1967.
Oil on canvas, 55 x 48 in.
The Parrish Art Museum, Gift of Jane Freilicher

39. *The Wood Road*. 1967-68.
Oil on canvas, 14 x 16 in.
The Parrish Art Museum,
Gift of the Estate of Fairfield Porter

40. *Self-Portrait in the Studio*. 1968.
Oil on Masonite, 22 x 16 in.
Private Collection, Stuart, Florida

41. *Columbus Day*. 1968.
Oil on canvas, 80 x 80 in.
Collection Dr. Marianne de Nagy Buchenhorner,
Courtesy Tibor de Nagy Gallery, New York

42. *Self-Portrait*. 1968.
Oil on canvas, 59 x 46 in.
Dayton Art Institute, Ohio, Museum Purchase
with funds provided by the National Endowment
for the Arts and various matching funds

43. *Boathouses and Lobster Pots*. 1968-72.
Oil on canvas, 48 x 60 in.
Mead Art Museum, Amherst College,
Amherst, Massachusetts, Museum Purchase

44. *Island Farmhouse*. 1969.
Oil on canvas, 80 x 79 in.
Private Collection, Cleveland, Ohio

45. *Amherst Campus No. 1*. 1969.
Oil on canvas, 62 x 46 in.
The Parrish Art Museum,
Gift of the Estate of Fairfield Porter

46. *Clearing Weather*. 1969.
Oil on canvas, 19 1/4 x 24 in.
The Parrish Art Museum,
Gift of the Estate of Fairfield Porter

47. *South Meadow from the Beach*. c. 1970.
Oil on canvas, 33 1/2 x 23 5/8 in.
The Parrish Art Museum,
Gift of the Estate of Fairfield Porter

48. *View of Barred Islands*. 1970.
Oil on canvas, 40 1/2 x 50 in.
Rose Art Museum, Brandeis University,
Waltham, Massachusetts, The Herbert W. Plimpton
Collection

49. *The Campus*. 1970.
Oil on canvas, 30 x 28 in.
The Parrish Art Museum,
Gift of the Estate of Fairfield Porter

50. *Portrait of a Girl*. 1971.
Oil on canvas, 41 1/4 x 27 3/8 in.
The Parrish Art Museum,
Gift of the Estate of Fairfield Porter

51. *Aline by the Screen Door*. 1971.
Oil on canvas, 55 x 48 in.
Collection Stephen S. Alpert, Boston,
Massachusetts.

52. *Under the Elms*. 1971.
Oil on canvas, 62 x 46 in.
Pennsylvania Academy of the Fine Arts,
Philadelphia, Gift of Mrs. Fairfield Porter

53. *Snow—South Main Street*. c. 1972.
Oil on paper mounted on board, 14 x 17 in.
The Phillips Collection, Washington, D.C.,
Anonymous Gift, 1992

54. *Late Afternoon—Snow*. c. 1972.
Oil on paper mounted on board, 14 x 17 in.
The Phillips Collection, Washington, D.C.,
Anonymous Gift, 1992

55. *Self-Portrait*. 1972.
Oil on canvas, 14 1/4 x 10 7/8 in.
The Parrish Art Museum
Gift of the Estate of Fairfield Porter

56. *The Ocean*. 1972.
Oil on canvas, 40 x 40 in.
Collection Arlie James Lambert,
Bristol, Tennessee

57. *The Beginning of the Fields*. 1973.
Oil on canvas, 52 x 76 in.
Memorial Art Gallery of the University of
Rochester, New York, Marion
Stratton Gould Fund

58. *Lizzie, Guitar and Christmas Tree, No. 1*. 1973.
Oil on canvas, 76 x 42 in.
The Parrish Art Museum,
Gift of the Estate of Fairfield Porter

59. *Sunrise on South Main Street*. 1973.
Oil on canvas, 43 x 55 in.
The Metropolitan Museum of Art, New York,
Hugo Kastor Fund, 1976

60. *The Dock*. 1974.
Oil on canvas, 20 x 36 in.
William A. Farnsworth Library and Art Museum,
Rockland, Maine, Gift of Anne Porter

61. *The Harbor—Great Spruce Head*. 1974.
Oil on canvas, 20 x 36 in.
Collection Andre Nasser, New York

62. *Blue Landscape*. 1974.
Oil on canvas, 45 1/2 x 45 1/2 in.
The Parrish Art Museum,
Gift of the Estate of Fairfield Porter

63. *Anne in Doorway*. 1974.
Oil on canvas, 47 x 37 in.
The Heckscher Museum, Huntington, New York
Gift of Mrs. Fairfield Porter

64. *Yellow Sunrise*. 1974.
Oil on canvas, 31 x 23 in.
Collection Katharine M. Porter, Atlanta, Georgia

65. The Privet Hedge. 1975.
Oil on Masonite, 18 x 22 in.
Private Collection, Courtesy Alpha Gallery, Boston,
Massachusetts

PHOTOGRAPHY CREDITS

In many cases, photographs have been provided by the owners or custodians of the works reproduced. The following list applies to those photographs for which a separate acknowledgment is due:

E. Irving Blomstrann (cat. no. 16)
Geoffrey Clements (cat. no. 25)
Eric Davis (cat. no. 65)
Bill Dewey (cat. no. 30)
Helga Photo Studio (cat. nos. 51, 56, 61)
David Henry (cat. no. 57)
Hirschl & Adler Modern (cat. nos. 22, 48)
Richard P. Meyer (cat. nos. 7, 10, 36, 49, 62)
David Preston (cat. no. 55)
Michael Price (cat. nos. 33, 40)
Nathan Rabin (cat. no. 18)
Adam Reich (cat. no. 8, 11, 21, 28, 29)
Noel Rowe (cat nos. 1, 2, 3, 4, 9, 13, 19, 23, 34, 37. 39, 46, 47, 50, 58)
Lee Stalsworth (cat. no. 12)
Jim Strong, Inc. (cat. nos. 5, 20, 31, 38, 45, 63)
Xystus Studio (cat. no. 6)

Library of CongressCatalog Card Number:
93-083244
ISBN 0-943526-25-6

Designed by Dana Levy, Perpetua Press, Los Angeles
Typeset and composed in Berkeley fonts on a
Mac II computer using Pagemaker software
Printed by Tien Wah Press, Singapore